FEARLESS CHANGE

Embrace the Choice to Reinvent Your Life

Judy Saalinger, Ph.D., MFT, CAS

Lasting Recovery Publications

Fearless Change

Embrace the Choice to Reinvent Your Life

Lasting Recovery Publications

6046 Cornerstone Court W. #112

San Diego, CA 92121

(800) 808-6373   ·

The case histories in this book are derived from actual interviews. The relevant facts are real, but all the names and other identifying details have been changed to protect the privacy of individuals. While the book discusses certain issues, situations and choices regarding therapy and other emotional healing work, it is not intended as a substitute for professional mental health advice.

ISBN # 0-9710272-0-X

This book is dedicated to

The Spirit of Change

*You have both broken and healed my
heart to bring grace into my life.
Thank you for your
miraculous gifts.*

The Process Works!

Table of Contents

Acknowledgements

I am forever thankful to my husband, Arthur, and daughter, Katie, for their love, endless encouragement, feedback, patience and support. And a thank you to Sela, a wonder and delight, whose steady love and support of our family keeps us in motion. And to my cousin, Stewart, for the push to write from my inner voice, his skill, love and light.

A special thank you to Wilna, a muse and wonderfully insightful woman who helped keep me on task with her love and kindness, patience and humor. Her editorial skills, artistic talents and gentle spirit are woven throughout these pages. Thanks also to her mother, Wendy, for her editorial skill.

Thanks go to attorney Peter Karlen for his ability to give a title to my work, and to the editors who have inspired me as I have learned to write from my inner voice: Judy Reeves, author of *A Writer's Book of Days*, Laurie Gibson for her excellence and skill, to Beverly Trainer for her ability to tweak a sentence, to Julie D. for her exquisite attention to detail, to Stephanie Gunning, for her warmth and humor, skill and insight, which helped me uncover my direction. Special appreciation to the rays of light in my life, Mary Goulet, Kathryn Davis-Finch, Kay McGavin, Judy Kaplan Baron, Beatrex Quintana, Lesah Beckhusen and Barbara Solis, who had faith from the beginning that I could and would complete this undertaking.

I am especially grateful to my clients for their valuable feedback during the development of this book and for sharing their journeys of Fearless Change with me.

Part One

"We cannot live a choice-less life.

Every day, every moment, every second

there is a choice. If it were not so

we would not be individuals."

— Ernest Holmes

Welcome

"You need chaos in your soul to give birth to a dancing star."

— Nietzsche

Congratulations. You've made one of the most incredible decisions in your life! To embrace the choice to reinvent your life will give you the most empowering skills you will ever know. Whether the current change in your life was initiated by you or visited upon you by something outside yourself, the following pages will open you to a new perspective on your inner self and the relationship to your life experiences. I invite you to see that the events of life are opportunities for us to find meaning and compassion as we learn effective ways to get our needs met.

Over the years I have seen that difficulty adjusting to change is one of the initial reasons why people make the phone call to begin therapy.

Reconstructing our lives to sustain recovery and heal from chemicals, relationships, divorce, illness, disability, career change, retirement or death often takes us into uncharted waters in our mind and soul. To find a new center of comfort often requires us to take a leap of faith along with a continuous effort to learn and integrate new ways of dealing with our emotions, our bodies and our dreams. Discovering our faith, we become fearless.

"Fearless Change" refers to the spirit of change as either God, spirit, higher power, silent love or the energy of creation. This spirit moves through life, bringing treasures unknown, yet is itself formless and changeless. The spirit of change knows no religious or cultural boundaries. This spirit is everlasting and eternal. The spirit of change doesn't evolve always the way we would imagine, but it does evolve for our highest good. To struggle and resist brings suffering, guilt, anger and sadness, whereas to accept change and surrender to its greater strength brings peace and balance.

I refer to the process of recovery throughout this book in a broad sense. To recover is to reclaim, recuperate, make progress, improve, mend, restore to health or regain some aspect of that which was lost. Recovery applies not only to the process of how we heal from the effects of addictions, but how we adapt and recover our sense of self when we have experienced any type of loss. The goal of recovery is to improve our strength and reclaim our sense of freedom and hope.

Below is a list of events, which are catalysts, sparks that ignite the energy necessary for us to grow and develop. Whether the change in your life involves attachment or separation, gaining or losing, birth or death, each one is a deep and powerful human event, a natural aspect of living in this physical world:

- Injury, illness or surgery
- Career change or setback
- Any change in diet
- Realization of the effects of addiction, in your own life or that of parents, partner, child, friend or co-worker
- Stopping any form of substance abuse
- Dissatisfaction with a close relationship
- The beginning or end of a friendship or relationship
- New romance, marriage or divorce
- Birth of a child or child leaving home
- Adoption or becoming a step or foster parent

- Taking on the care of an aging parent(s)
- Separation from partner or friends
- Return to an old behavior or thought process
- A family member going into or out of recovery
- New religious or spiritual views
- Starting a creative project
- Inheritance
- Bankruptcy
- A change in residence
- Beginning or completion of your education
- Issues with midlife or aging
- Death of a family member, friend, or pet
- An urge to try--or the fear of--something new

Whatever, however, whenever change is manifesting in your life, know that within the following pages you'll discover some essential tools to transform your perceptions and responses. You'll learn to focus on the positive possibilities to create joy and fulfillment. You are now ready to begin the journey to reinvent your life!

FEARLESS CHANGE MAP

HUMAN NEEDS **INTERDEPENDENT** **UNIVERSE**

Physical	Safety	Communication	Energy of Creation
Love	Belonging	Inner Voice	People
Self Esteem	Others Esteem	Outer Voice	Places
Understanding	Knowledge	Listening	Things
Aesthetics	Self Actualization	Boundaries	Time

LIFE EXPERIENCES IN GETTING NEEDS MET

 CHOICES

PATH OF FEAR	PATH OF TRUST
DENY / RESIST →	**ACCEPT**
COMMUNICATION **PASSIVE AGGRESSIVE** Thoughts / Emotions / Responses	**COMMUNICATION** **ASSERTIVE** Thoughts / Emotions / Responses
CONTROL	**COOPERATE**

REFRAME

Path of Fear — CONTROL		Path of Trust — COOPERATE	
SELF	**OTHERS**	**SELF**	**OTHERS**
ISOLATE DENY NEEDS ADDICTION	BLAME DEFEND MANIPULATE	LISTEN TO INNER VOICE	DETACH NEGOTIATE TEAM PLAYER

HELPLESS / STRESSED	**TAKE ACTION**

ANGER / RESENTMENTS →	**CREATE SOLUTIONS**
INWARD	**OUTWARD**	**INWARD**	**OUTWARD**

INWARD	OUTWARD	INWARD	OUTWARD
ILLNESS DEPRESSION	VIOLENT AGGRESSIVE	EMPOWERED ESTEEMED	CONFIDENT NEED SATISFIED
SUICIDE **DEATH**	**RAGE** **RELAPSE**	**SECURE** **TRUST**	**LIVE OUR** **VISION**

www.LastingRecovery.com

Chapter 1

Fearless Change Map

"The great thing in this world is not so much where we are,
but in what direction we are moving."

—Oliver Wendell Holmes

This map is your guide to Fearless Change. Study it, know it and learn to use it. At all times and in all situations, you will find yourself either on the Path of Trust or the Path of Fear. The goal is to live as many days as you can on the Path of Trust, enjoying life and fielding change with grace and dignity. During my years of working with clients (as well as on myself), I developed the Fearless Change Map to help us better understand the impact of change on our consciousness.

In the early 1970s I was married, lived in a big house and was happily settling into the domestic scene. Still in my twenties, I'd already landed a challenging and lucrative job. I started putting money into a retirement account, bought life insurance and some property on which to build a retirement home. I was just waiting to start my family. Everything seemed to be going right according to *my* schedule. Then the elusive spirit of change arrived on the scene.

I first became aware of the power of change when my mother was diagnosed with lung cancer. She died five weeks later. Addicted to cigarettes, her illness had been brewing for forty years. I was devastated. I couldn't work or sleep. I wandered around in a daze, lost and crying whenever I thought of her. I felt as if my foundation had been blown apart. The whole world looked like a cemetery. The family home was empty without her love and energy. The school where Mother had taught eighth-graders, once so alive and vibrant, now seemed desolate.

If that weren't enough, our family pets began to die, one after the other. And still more unexpected change appeared: Both my grandparents, with whom I was very close, died within eighteen months of Mother's death. My sweet, gentle grandmother had loved me unconditionally. Now she, the light of my life, was gone. Grandpa, quiet, funny and a wonderful role model of commitment and love, was no longer there to hear about my adventures, to share apple pie and ice cream, or to tell me not to take any wooden nickels. Gone were the family historians who remembered the early years and told stories of how we had evolved as a family.

The feeling of loss was so overwhelming that a chronic back problem suddenly worsened. I had trouble working and went on disability. I was diagnosed as having incurable pain in my spine, and the doctor prescribed that antiquated all-purpose solution for ailing women—a hysterectomy. Now there would never be children to fill the empty rooms of our spacious home or to add life to the family tree. I felt suspended in space, severed from humanity. Most of all, I didn't feel like a *real woman*.

The way my father coped with my mother's death was to remarry, sell the family home and move away. At first I was glad that he was moving on with his life, until I received a photocopied letter that was sent to my three brothers and me. Its message was terse: *"Now that your mother is dead and I have remarried, I will be spending time with my new wife and her family. I wish you well in your life. – Dad."* I felt orphaned. There would be no more birthday cards or parties, and no more Christmas or Thanksgiving celebrations. I was on my own.

I was struck by the differences between my life and that of my friends. Seven of them were healthy, pregnant, happily employed and blessed with relatives surrounding them. At first I tried to deny that my life had been turned upside down, and then I woke up one morning and decided to get a divorce, move out of town, go back to school and start a new life. Some people said I simply "snapped." Like my dad, I decided to exchange the world I had known for the promise of a new beginning.

I called a few friends and told them I was moving. I said good-bye to my mother-in-law, and hugged my sobbing and confused husband. Packing up my yellow VW with my dog, some clothes, my inheritance of family dishes, a few pieces of jewelry, a blanket from my grandfather and one filled with the scent of my mother's perfume, I headed out in search of a fresh start. I had no idea how it was going to unfold and I was appropriately scared. I was leaving the structure my family and society had created for women: get married, establish a home, have children, work part-time to fulfill yourself, retire, travel, grow old with your grandkids and die in peace. Having abandoned all that, I was now venturing into uncharted territory. I was as frightened as I was excited.

And so the foundation of the Fearless Change Map was born. I realized that I needed to find other ways to fulfill my needs for family, vocation, giving and receiving love, trust and personal expression. The bottom line was that I needed a reason to keep living.

I began to rethink my expectations about my mom and dad, what I believed I needed from them, and what I was going to miss. I knew my three brothers loved me, but they had their own lives. Whatever it was I thought I needed, I certainly wasn't going to get it from my family. I had to explore other ways to become whole again.

I moved fifty miles away and enrolled in college. I found a roommate and started to explore this new beginning. One day while I was unpacking and setting up housekeeping in my new apartment, I had a sudden surge of feeling—almost like being reborn. I was so alive I could almost feel the energy crackling around me.

This was the era when college campuses were hotbeds of change. I met new people, made friends and became involved in the consumer rights movement. It was a time of change for the world as well as for me. Like many of my peers, I rebelled against established traditions. We fought the good fight for women's rights, and signed our name with a flourishing "*Ms.*" Caught up in the wildness and passion of youth, we hitchhiked across the country and all through Europe, exposed our brains to a variety of drugs and experimented romantically as we welcomed in the sexual revolution. We thumbed our nose at the taboos of the tribe, seeking new levels of emotional and spiritual awareness. We tried meditation, sensitivity groups and magic mushrooms. We wanted things to be different and weren't afraid to do whatever it took to bring about change. We were the hope of the future, unlike any generation before us.

Then things slowed down.

The war in Vietnam was over, and our soldiers returned home, forever marked by the horrors of that controversial conflict. Laws were enacted to protect consumers, the Civil Rights Act had been passed and Ms. was now a household word. The country settled into a new comfort zone, and I put away my picket sign. I graduated from college, married again, changed my name and traded in my worn-out Levis and Salvation Army tee-shirt for a polyester pants suit. I took a corporate job and began teaching consumer economics at a community college. The party was over, and now those of us who'd battled the establishment and never trusted anyone over 30 suddenly found ourselves members of the club. It all seemed so prescribed and automatic to return to the framework of my earlier life.

But I missed the excitement and camaraderie of those heady college days. The thrills provided by those adventurous times had simply postponed my grieving process. Now I found myself reeling from the uprooting of my life, and the unresolved loss of my family. It wasn't long before I began to feel overwhelmingly afraid, and my fears escalated into full-blown panic attacks. My creative and emotional energy was depleted. I once felt powerful when I battled big business and the government—and when I thought I could make a difference saving the world. But when it came time to save myself, I gave up because I didn't know how or where to begin.

I was hopelessly passive. I couldn't communicate what I felt because I didn't *know* what I felt. Instead I tried to keep up a happy front, but in reality I'd bottled up all my creative energy because I didn't know where or how to use it. Finally I became depressed and sick, simply burned out. I tried to carry on in spite of what was going on with my body, but I knew I had to reinvent my life.

At this point I was on the left side of the Fearless Change Map. I wanted to control the change by moving on to something new, yet I had not fully grieved or let go of the multiple losses in my life. I was in total denial. My body began to shut down. I could barely walk across the room and my energy was gone. I felt depressed, lost and, most of all, powerless. The physical pain I endured was compounded by my pent-up emotions. The tranquilizers and pain pills I had been given to mask the pain were deadening my mind. I began to question what I really felt. Being drugged up as a zombie didn't seem to make life any better. I wanted and needed to do something differently.

It was at this point that I began the process of reframing my life. I was talking to my friend, Patti, and told her how overwhelmed I felt. Hoping to find some clue that might lead to a solution, Patti and I looked up the word *fear* in the dictionary to find the antonym: *faith*. Staring at that word on the printed page made me feel I'd found my answer!

I began reading about people whose faith had helped them become more open to healing. Some of them had created powerful changes in their lives by realizing they had a choice: They could continue in pain or learn to heal their thoughts and feelings without drugs. Those who had healed learned to accept reality, rather than remaining unhappy over the unmet expectations that had caused their anger and sadness. They learned to forgive others. They learned to pray and trust the power of the universe. Most wrote about newly discovered aspects of themselves. Many of these people had grown stronger despite what they had been through. They had healed their lives, bodies, finances and their relationships. All the people I read about learned to love and forgive themselves unconditionally, regardless of what others had said or done. They told themselves they were healthy and whole and spent time visualizing the light of love surrounding every aspect of their bodies.

The books I read challenged me to focus on God, the spirit of creation, rather than any specific problem. After I explored the many facets of healing, studied spiritual and motivational books, listened to meditation tapes, prayed, meditated and attended services to learn all the ways people honor the power and presence of God in their everyday life, I slowly began changing my perceptions.

I became mindful of life around me—aware of the present moment. I made the decision to become fully conscious each morning as I went about getting out of bed, brushing my teeth, and preparing and eating my breakfast. I concentrated on each step I took, each motion of my hands, and each conscious thought. I said aloud, *I am aware that my left foot is touching the ground, I am aware that my right foot is touching the ground, I am aware that I am picking up the cup, I am aware that I am pouring the water.* I began to feel the presence of spirit in the work I did, the way I took a breath, the way I moved. I began to increase my awareness of a lot of things I'd previously ignored. I learned that I could change the words I said to myself, and consequently change how I felt. When I recalled memories, I could reframe them, and from there I could change my outlook.

What was most amazing was that I discovered that by changing just one word in my inner dialogue, I could change my attitude. Instead of thinking of painful outcomes, I began to repeat the word *faith*. I chose to become aware of and to trust the laws of the universe that I already accepted. I could trust the sun to come up, the fact that rain was composed of water and not oil, and the laws of gravity. As my trust increased, I learned about assertiveness, which simply means to ask nicely and directly for what you want.

When I learned that I had to ask for what I wanted in relationships with men, I was upset. I thought that if a man really loved me, he should just *know* what I needed. If he got it right, then it must be true love. But if he happened to guess wrong, it meant he didn't love me and I stayed empty. As a champion of the downtrodden, I'd had no trouble demanding rights for others, but I'd never been taught how to ask for myself.

During this time I also learned that my higher power was the one who really loved me—totally and unconditionally. I realized that when I trusted my *spirit*, my need was met even if my desires were unclear. I would "listen" on a deep level, and trust the answer to unfold. As understanding came, I began to interpret the messages of pain, tension and so-called coincidences. I was open to inner guidance in the form of intuition or a spiritual nudge. I learned to forgive my judgments against others, both in the present and in my past.

I was able to ask this all-powerful spirit for everything I needed. Then I followed with action, believing the need would be fulfilled as long as I listened to my inner promptings and maintained my faith and perseverance. Daily, for months, I visualized this energy of light, fire, destruction and creation moving in and through my body and mind. I affirmed in thoughts, images and in words that I was already strong and healthy. Eventually the words and feelings were submerged in my unconscious and I began to have calm and pain-free days, dreams of peace and feelings of strength.

In short—it worked! At last I could access the calm center of my being and know what it meant to be pain-free. At first it was for only a few fleeting minutes, then for longer periods of time. I was starting to feel stronger and healthier, just as I had affirmed. I had successfully moved my perception from fear to trust, on the right-hand side of the chart. With fear there was darkness, weakness, depression and pain. With trust, I experienced light, strength, vision and new beginnings.

I began to research how my experiences might help others. After becoming a therapist and talking to literally thousands of people over the years in therapy, workshops and on the radio, I realized that legions of people had the same problems I did. I wasn't alone.

I have since used the Fearless Change Map with clients in therapy and in workshops. This map will help you in the same way it's helped them to understand the elements of anger, change, powerlessness, boundaries, communication and a multitude of other issues. The Fearless Change Map is a mirror of your inner self. You can see where you're headed and where you want to be. Use it as your compass. Trust in the journey of Fearless Change.

Look over the Fearless Change Map on page 6. Our basic needs are interdependent on our environment, including the universe of people, places, things, time and the energy of creation. The fulfillment of these needs is based on our ability to communicate with the universe through our verbal and non-verbal interactions.

The next section, our Life Experiences in Getting Our Needs Met, reflects the beliefs, expectations and perceptions we have today. We acquire certain characteristics from our relationships, families and communities. These characteristics protect our most inner, vulnerable self, and are based on prior experiences, values, personality type, families of origin and our soul's purpose.

If we believe in the possibilities within the universe to have our needs met, we can approach change with trust. We accept what is in front of us, cooperate with it and take the necessary actions. We have satisfied our immediate need and met our soul's requirement to grow. If, on the other hand, we resist change and growth, it may be because we have unrealistic expectations of who we are or how our lives *ought* to be. We may feel disappointment, shame or guilt because our bodies, relationships, children, jobs or investments don't respond as we think they should. We then develop a fearful perspective and we become defensive and rigid, either externally or internally. If we try to shut down our emotions, we become ill, get depressed, open ourselves to addictions, become enraged or relapse. We propel ourselves right into emotional or physical burnout. When we act out our defensiveness externally, we become angry, irritable, sarcastic or manipulative. Many people show their passive side to the world while churning inside with fear and rage.

The sooner we choose to reframe our negative beliefs into empowering thoughts, the more quickly our trust returns and we can accept the change at hand. We can then access our creative instincts and seek a solution. Some answers appear effortlessly and others may take continual revisiting, depending on the depth of pain and trauma. Reframing the change through our thoughts, words, breathing and actions allows us to collect our thoughts, imagine a positive outcome and accept what is in front of us right now.

Think about a major change going on in your life today. Locate your position on the map, then decide which process you want to engage in: the problem or the solution. Follow the suggestions in this book and allow yourself to be reinvented through the path to Fearless Change. ⊱

Chapter 2

Facing the Unknown

"Do not follow where the path may lead,
go instead where there is no path and leave a trail."

—Ralph Waldo Emerson

Do you find that you get anxious when you even *think* of making changes? Or do you worry that other people's transformations are going to affect you? Some changes we can influence; others we have no control over; and still others we try to avoid. When our expectations have been challenged and we're not the one making the decisions, it's natural to feel out of control. We can kick and scream, or we can choose to see change as a reflection of our inner growth, and use the power of our thoughts and choices to make empowering decisions. Either way, we must realize we have chosen experiences and relationships to challenge us and give our soul an opportunity to develop. Then, when we've learned the needed lesson, our soul urges us to move on.

One of the first lessons I had to learn was that if I wanted things to be different, I first had to accept reality. *Actual* reality, not just my "wouldn't-it-be-nice-if" version. Reality is shaped by our expectations, and we usually have no awareness of this principle until it's challenged. When I examined the impact of my fear of abandonment, poverty, criticism and illness on my perception of reality, I realized that the fear of abandonment by my mother had become a reality, and I worried about my own old age and death.

In some situations we expect the best and other times the worst. When we're aware of what we are thinking, including our expectations and fears, we can constructively direct our thoughts, actions and responses into the void of the unknown. I finally realized that when I'm needy, it's *my* responsibility to discover beneficial ways to validate my self-worth. Otherwise, I end up depending on others to make me feel whole. When I give someone or something else the power to make me feel complete—which I already am—I sacrifice an aspect of my personal worth. If I believe that it's not "nice" for me to get my way or say "no," I've given up my power to ask for what I want or to protect my values and vulnerability.

Reinventing ourselves as we go through change means redesigning our self-concept. We can help find the necessary strength by identifying our thoughts and turning them around to be prayerful and positive. When we're aware of our needs, thoughts, words, feelings and actions, we're then able to respond from our higher self and move with grace. And then opportunities start to reveal themselves. We're invited to have new experiences, and we willingly say "yes" to the new leg of our life adventure. We begin to see ourselves differently as we try new roles, take on new responsibilities and see life from a perspective of living fully, free from past pain or the need for approval.

Our lives are in constant flux as we adapt to our powerlessness in controlling the flow in this great universe. Our only *real* power is in our response to change. Think of a change you overcame in the past and what you did to rebalance and grow through the process. Remember, you wouldn't be *here* if you hadn't been *there*.

With the keys to Fearless Change you'll discover a positive and creative solution no matter what the challenge. Take the time now to reflect on whatever transformation is going on in your life. We need to relate to the change if we're going to manage it and move to the next phase. Change has a rippling effect, impacting other areas of our lives as well as those close to us. You may be going through several changes all at once, and if so, concentrate — right now — on the one that's most challenging. Sit for a few minutes and get clear on how to describe it. Then explain in detail:

1. What's the most challenging change you're facing?

2. What excites you most about this change?

3. What do you fear most about the change?

4. Describe a time in the past when you experienced significant change.

5. How did you move beyond it to rebalance your life?

6. What benefits were derived from that change?

7. What do you think you can learn from this current change —
about yourself? About others?

8. Are you willing to trust the outcome inherent in this change?

By fully answering these questions now, you'll receive the greatest benefit from this book, and should immediately begin to see change from a new perspective. Learning Fearless Change Choices will enable you to face the unknown with confidence.

Chapter 3

What We Believe

"It's not the events of our lives that shape us,
but our beliefs as to what those events mean."

— Anthony Robbins

Our beliefs and behavior about the change have considerable power in determining how we let go of what was in our life and move with faith toward the outcome of the new. The perception we have about our abilities to maintain our sobriety, keep our food plan, love again, and recover from illness or injury, is revealed to us through our trust or resistance in moving forward. Trusting the process of change and growth is not always easy as we reflect on our prior experiences, and hear in the backgrounds of our minds the voices of our family, culture and community.

The Characteristics of Relationships Chart on the next page shows the varying dynamics within our families, partnerships, friendships, workplaces and neighborhoods. When we understand the thought patterns and actions that bind us to our old way of being, we are truly free to grow. As we shift our concentration from fears held over from our past to trusting images and ideas, we move the flow of energy in our lives from negative to positive. The following lists describe the beliefs and behaviors we reveal in our day-to-day lives as we relate to people and situations.

Check off the current qualities of either fear or trust that are in your life today.

Characteristics

Fear / Shame / Pain-Based

____ Feels jealousy, suspicion and mistrust
____ Unaffectionate
____ Believes God is punishing and judgmental
____ Feels unrealistic guilt
____ Rejects or resists change
____ Doesn't set goals — Why be disappointed?
____ Sees life as chaotic, unsafe
____ Emotional pain is denied, ignored
____ Mistakes are failures, "must do perfectly"
____ Would feel too guilty to say "no"
____ Not safe to tell the truth
____ Voice silenced — not able to protect self
____ Individuation discouraged
____ Damaged boundaries, reactive, defensive
____ Reacts, distorts, creates distance
____ Believes responsible FOR each other
____ Control, limitations
____ Autocratic — "Do it my way or else."
____ Unrealistic expectations
____ Conditional love
____ Inner child feels discouraged
____ Low self-esteem
____ Denial

Check off the beliefs, attitudes or behaviors you'd like to embrace on your journey of Fearless Change.

Characteristics

Trust / Love / Pleasure-Based

___ Feels love, trusting and safe
___ Demonstrates affection
___ Believes God unconditionally loves
___ Feels innocent
___ Open to the new, different
___ Sets goals — motivates self and becomes a model to others
___ Sees life as safe and in divine order
___ Emotional pain is accepted
___ Mistakes are for learning
___ Able to set boundaries, say "no"
___ Truth is spoken
___ Voice expressed — uses negotiation skills
___ Individuation encouraged
___ Clear boundaries — healthy defenses
___ Responds, listens, creates intimacy
___ Believes responsible TO each other
___ Freedom to risk and try
___ Democratic — "Let's reach mutual decision."
___ Accepts reality
___ Unconditional love
___ Inner child feels encouraged
___ High self-esteem
___ Recovery

I used to live my life according to many of the fear-based list of characteristics, and I have found that most of my clients have too. One of the pleasures of being a therapist is to watch a person discover the joy of learning to trust and finally accept themselves just as they are. Or seeing their eyes filled with excitement as they talk about understanding more of their own motivations, setting healthy boundaries in their relationships, taking actions on their own or being aware of the synchronistic events in their lives. I love seeing the smile when they recognize that the tragedy that had brought them pain carried within it the seed of their new beginning. Moving from fear to trust-based characteristics takes time, an awareness of our choices and the development of our faith.

In the early part of my healing I didn't believe in anything greater than myself; I had fear, shame and pain-based characteristics. I knew I had to seriously examine my thoughts if I was going to experience a pain-free and drug-free body that to me would be the foundation of a rewarding life. Many of my friends seemed to love and trust themselves and express more natural, pleasure-based characteristics. They validated themselves, took vacations, spent time in their kitchens and gardens and basically enjoyed themselves and the simple pleasures in life. I loved myself "conditionally" and frequently told myself, "I could love you if only _____ were different." I'd frequently give myself a little dig when I didn't do something perfectly or felt deprived.

I was afraid most of the time as I ventured into new arenas. I feared making the wrong decisions and, as a result, I put my life on hold. I worried about everything from whether I was unloved, would burn the dinner or wrap my car around a telephone pole. I didn't trust anything or anybody and the images in my mind were less than beautiful. I realized I'd been scared for a very long time. I didn't want to feel the pain again, nor did I want to use substances to mask my needs. Seeking a relationship with my inner aspect — that part of me untouched by the events of my life — seemed the only way out.

As I look around today, I'm amazed that my life is so full and satisfying. Since I've begun to discover my own potential, I have so much to be grateful for. But these things didn't just "appear" in my life. I realized I had choices, that I was not helpless and, as I embraced growth, I began seeing the positive experiences in life. I learned to trust, make wiser decisions and choices and became more cooperative, understanding and satisfied.

Developing Trust

The first change was learning to believe in a higher power. By acting *as if* I could trust, I began to have faith. I started to understand that I'd unconsciously absorbed qualities, reactions and feelings from my experiences growing up and living in the world.

During my meditation I visualized the pure light within me burning up the old belief that I couldn't have a pain-free body, love, family and prosperity. This gave me the freedom to start each day choosing positive thoughts, and allowed me to ask the universe for fulfillment. I was beginning to understand that *if we don't ask, we don't receive.* I affirmed that I would be successful in creating a life filled with physical strength, love, trust, pleasure and meaning.

Every day we make a multitude of decisions that affect whether we will feel trust or fear. I've since come to understand that when we're struggling with a decision, however large or small, we fall into self-doubt, the seedling of fear. With this doubt comes inaction and we stay stuck. To gather courage during this time of change, I practiced meditation and self-hypnosis to quiet my mind and asked for guidance. We need to keep ourselves in the creative flow of life to receive the answers we need. That feeling of apprehension begins to surface when we don't have enough information to trust that we'll be safe during our journey.

What I finally learned was that if I only saw what was *right with me*, then I'd only see what was right with other people or situations. When I dwelled on my imperfections, I was still clinging to my old fear-based belief system. When I judged others, I was judging myself, because people serve as mirrors. What I liked or disliked, did or didn't want, had or didn't have, was reflected right back at me through my perceptions. Our inner voice can create joy when we embrace self-acceptance, forgiveness and enthusiasm. Feeling unconditional love toward ourselves, the foundation of solid self-esteem, makes it easier for us to see the world as a safe place. Creating high self-esteem results from stretching to reach our most inspired potential, and not giving up, no matter what!

Embrace Your Fears

Somewhere along my healing journey I recall hearing that there were six fears that ruled peoples lives, leading them to develop fear and shame-based characteristics: the fear of poverty, criticism, illness, loss of love, fear of aging and death. Growing up in families where there is abuse, trauma, addiction and abandonment creates uncertainty and mistrust in the power of others to provide us with trust, love and feelings of safety. Through putting more energy on strengthening the emotional sensation of trust we can overcome those old characteristics, which encompassed our lives.

The fear of poverty, of lack and threats to our survival often affect us during times of change. Although common, these fears are destructive because our sense of self is undermined. Fearing poverty, we worry even as we become indifferent to our needs, and we lose our sense of imagination and enthusiasm. We feel helpless and little. This fear causes us to doubt our abilities, become over-cautious, procrastinate and either rationalize our failures or envy those who have succeeded in moving forward. To overcome this anxiety we need to tap into our associated memories, and develop a more positive relationship with the idea of prosperity and of money. Affirming the abundance of people, ideas and opportunities in the world, we can be assured that if we are open to take responsibility for our choices and then are willing to receive, the universe is there to provide.

Carolyn, a dear friend of mine, was overwhelmed with fears of poverty. Her parents had divorced when she was young and many nights she went to bed hungry and lonely. Even though she was making an adequate salary as an elementary school teacher, and had taken care of the physical aspects of her money through studying books on financial planning, she felt poor. Her church offered a class on prosperity to work with the emotional and spiritual aspects of this divine energy. She became aware of her surroundings each day, the abundance of nature and slowly gained a feeling of prosperity in the world.

Another fear that blocks our growth is the dread of criticism. Many of us having been criticized in our families for making mistakes as we learned, or were judged harshly for not being perfect. Fearing criticism, we may deny our initiative and self-expression and curtail our imagination. If we uncover the source of our shame—being who we are—we reclaim our inner strength. The courage of self-expression is essential to good communication, which in turn brings confidence and self-esteem.

Thomas was in my office the other day with his wife. She was complaining that he seemed indifferent to family matters, and that, frankly, she was fed up with having to make all the decisions. After I asked Thomas a few questions, he confessed that he was afraid of conflict, so expressing no opinion seemed safer than having a controversial one. Raised in an alcoholic and abusive family, he had learned to just go along in order to avoid upsets. The mere thought of conflict made him shudder. After discussing some of the characteristics of adults who have been raised in toxic home environments, Thomas was able to understand that withholding himself was an old survival skill that he could now safely shed. Before the session was over, he was able to name three specific things he wanted in his relationship with his wife, and she seemed to show more respect for this husband she was just starting to really know.

Disappointments in relationships and careers may cause us to worry about the effects of change on our health. But often we discover that fearful thinking is our worst ailment. We can enjoy an abundance of well-being if our inner thoughts reflect health and wholeness, and if our daily actions support physical and emotional health. As we develop faith in the divine healer within, and acknowledge the abundance of both alternative and medical solutions, we can change our thinking.

Charlotte, a woman in one of my groups, complained of severe migraine headaches. They had started around the time her wealthy mother had written her out of her will because she disliked Charlotte's husband. Through exploring her thinking, her needs and beliefs, Charlotte realized that she'd always done what her mother had wanted, except when she married Peter. Without her mother's financial help, Charlotte feared she wouldn't be able to take care of herself, and in her later years, she might end up alone and sick. Her obsession over this fear manifested itself in the form of headaches and isolation. By learning some relaxation techniques and ways to think more positively, Charlotte was able to visualize a glowing light of radiant health in and through her body. Soon Charlotte's creativity awakened and she began to pursue her love of graphic arts. And in time she realized that her mother had actually given her something more precious than an inheritance—the freedom to think for herself. With her new enthusiasm for life, it was easier for her to create a balance of exercise, meditation and rewarding work.

When change fosters fears about loss of love, we become jealous, judgmental and, through lack of control, we often make poor financial decisions. We cannot force anyone to love us. The more loving and respectful we are toward ourselves and our dreams, the more love we receive in return.

Howard had to learn about the connection between money and love the hard way. He had come to see me several years ago because his wife had left him for another man, taking their daughters with her. He struggled with why she left and felt especially pained since he felt his mother had never really shown him love or affection. Howard was determined to change his life and ended up spending about seven years courting different women, buying them gifts, taking them out to dinner and on vacations. He wasn't a wealthy man, but he spent most of his earnings trying to buy love. When the last of his many relationships failed, he returned to therapy to sort out what had gone wrong. Making the connection between fearing that he was unloved and poor money management (as well as neglect for his car, his home and his body), Howard began to make new choices. He demonstrated love for himself by taking care of his health, his possessions and his financial future.

Almost all of us have some fear of old age and death. Our concerns about our twilight years result from collected images based on our experiences and beliefs. We can choose to envision spending more time enjoying the beauty of everyday life and someday passing over to greater peace. Charles Darwin said it wasn't the strongest or the most intelligent who survive the longest, but those who adapt well to change. Studies of those who live past the century mark prove this to be true.

My friend Sandy's grandmother took up hiking at age 76, after her husband died, and she went on week-end treks with her new hiking club until she was 87. She's still active in the hiking club and takes advantage of their shorter walks. My dad was afraid of dying before he was 50, as neither of his parents lived beyond their forties. Once he passed that significant birthday, he got involved in the Navy League as a volunteer, helping men and women in military service who were away from home. He also took up organ lessons and became a docent at his local train museum. He is 89 now, still drives and continues to be involved with friends who celebrate organ music and serve others. I think he is one of those survivors Darwin was talking about! So embrace your fears and accept the choices of Fearless Change!

What Are My Fears?

Poverty	_____	Criticism	_____
Illness	_____	Loss of Love	_____
Growing Older	_____	Death	_____

Describe other fears you sometimes experience:

Write out statements that affirm the direction in which you'd like to grow. You may wish to pass on this one, as dealing with this issue is not easy. But remember: Trust comes when we have information. So go ahead, pick up your pen and replace your fears with positive affirmations. For example:

Common Fears	**Is Reframed, for example, as:**
Fear of Poverty	*I am learning about managing and investing my money.*
Fear of Criticism	*I allow myself to be self - expressive.*
Fear of Illness	*I experience wellness in my body and all areas of my life.*
Fear of Loss of Love	*I love, honor and respect myself first, and others love me for me.*
Fear of Aging	*My awareness is deeper than my body. I am more mature and wise with each passing year.*
Fear of Death	*I am transitioning into greater peace and divine love.*

Congratulations! Rethinking just one thought is the first move toward a solution. By repeating an affirmation, and gently finessing the conflicting thought into agreement, your fears will begin to diminish.

Trust-Based Affirmations

Until I began affirming the possibilities of living a different life, I kept playing the old tapes in my mind. My outer voice would affirm, *I am living a wonderful life filled with great health, strength, love, laughter, family and a great sense of purpose. All is well.* Then my inner voice would argue, *You're a dreamer. Get real, you can't do that!* Or: *Go ahead and dream about it, but what's going to happen if you can't have it? What if you get it and then don't want it? You'll have wasted your energy, time and money.* One day, in a rather dramatic gesture, I wrote out all my old inner-voice beliefs and transformed their energy by burning the paper they were written on! A bit theatrical perhaps, but it worked for me. Until I released the old, my outer voice was invalidated by the cautions of my inner self. Now I was no longer blocking the light of the new. Now, real change could make its grand entrance.

Ever since I began healing feelings of deprivation by affirming health and a life filled with friends, laughter and ideas, my world has been changing for the good. I now use affirmations to regain my inner and outer balance. I've finally learned to live from the inside out, rather than the outside in. I've learned to reframe my thoughts, recognize coincidences as messages and allow my higher power to provide insight. Whenever I'm seeking an answer, I ask the spirit for guidance. Then, in a heightened state of awareness, I'm more apt to notice a significant coincidence, or focus on a book, or make or receive a call to someone who will tell me what I need to know.

If I'm resistant to something, I reflect on my feelings and beliefs about the situation. Then I ask whether or not the thought is useful in creating positive energy. If it isn't, I know I need to create another way of looking at things. Once I accept something, I have transformed my energy from negative to neutral. I am now free to make a choice: I can either recreate negative thoughts and images or use my energy to think and feel in a positive way.

It's amazing how the 26 letters of the alphabet, rearranged, can change our life. I have to work on some beliefs time and again as they continue to resurface. Having reinforced my self-imposed limitations at least 50,000 times, I now require at least 50,001 instances of highlighting the truth: There are unlimited possibilities!

My friend Mary used to believe that her partner should validate her self-esteem through his responses to her actions. Now she knows that she is the only one who can truly influence her self-esteem, by taking risks, giving herself approval, gaining confidence in her skills, setting boundaries and being assertive. She now believes her needs are important, and takes care of them in various ways. She makes the appointment with the dentist or the masseuse, and asks her family to pitch in at breakfast and lunch so she'll have time to greet the sunrise with a morning walk.

Changing our beliefs is akin to learning a new language. It takes commitment to follow through, even when we're not in the mood. In changing our thoughts, feelings and images, it's important to first state the words "I am." Right now, take a minute and say, "I am (your name)." Feel yourself centered deep inside by stating your given name. Recall your facial expressions and body language when you feel peaceful. Now, as you reframe your thoughts in a positive way, begin with "I am," and state your goal as if your are experiencing it this moment. Practice this new thought and feeling. What you are stating may not be the way you feel right now. But remember that this is a new language and way of being, and it takes time to overcome old habits. As the Nike saying goes, *Just Do It!*

Mind and Emotions

It's now time to set an objective for the first stage of your goal. Trust the words of your affirmations and take action. Some people develop a plan, and others just do it spontaneously. This is where most people get hung up. They don't truly believe they can accomplish their goal. Or they make a few attempts, and then quit. The truth is that we don't usually change unless we have sufficient motivation. Remind yourself of your incentive. Is it to avoid the pain of the past or is it to embrace the pleasure of the moment and the future? At each point in time we are making choices.

Of course it's easier to change our beliefs when there's the promise of a greater reward. For example, if you were asked to work the night shift, you might resist, saying you couldn't possibly alter your sleeping/waking schedule. Yet if your boss agreed to increase your pay and give you a promotion and your loved ones weren't too bothered by it, you might find it easier to make the necessary accommodations. Your thoughts change when there is a benefit involved.

Research shows that by age 15, 75 percent of children are negative thinkers. Impulses curtailed by the rules and limitations of parents, teachers, and society all impact on our perceptions. Emotions and behavior then respond to our restricted thoughts. Our mind and emotions always influence our thinking, whether it is positive or negative.

The secret to manifesting what you say to yourself is an emotional vibration attached to your words. Some people like to sing their affirmations to a favorite tune. The *Happy Birthday* song is one that tunes into our inner happy child and tunes out shame and judgment.

> *I am whole and complete.*
> *I am whole and complete.*
> *I trust and surrender.*
> *To the voice of silent love.*

If you commit your empowering affirmations to the emotional level of music and experience, your conscious awareness will evolve more quickly. It may seem like a lot of effort to expend on something you're not yet sure about. But if you *believe* that you're worth a mere ten minutes a day, you'll do it.

You can make even faster progress if you spend an hour or two a day for the next six months, and you don't even have to take time out of your current schedule. You can do affirmations when you wake up, while you're in the shower, driving, walking around your home or office, cooking or eating dinner, or waiting in the checkout line. After just a few days of working with these affirmations, you'll begin to notice that something's different. Keep a notebook or use the *Fearless Change Journal* to record the signs you experience that make the affirmation true. For example:

Affirmation:	Evidence:
I am feeling love and trust.	I woke up this morning and my cat was purring next to my head. The sun came up. I trust the world is on schedule.
I am open to the new.	I went to a new support group meeting today.

Affirmations for you:
> *I am feeling love and trust.*
> *I am open to the new and the different.*
> *I am setting goals; my thoughts create the possible.*
> *I see life as safe and in divine order.*

I am accepting my emotional pain. To feel is to heal.
I am accepting of my mistakes and see them as opportunities to learn and grow.
I set boundaries and allow myself to receive.
I am honest with others and myself.
I am expressing my opinions and beliefs.
I am who I am, separate from the roles I play.
I am able to set limits and communicate them to others.
I am responsive to others.
I am able to create intimacy with others through listening.
I am responsible to others – not for others.
I am free to risk and try new things.
I am making wise decisions.
I am accepting of life as it is today.
I allow love to flow through me. I resist not.
I am encouraged and I encourage others.
I love and I approve of myself.
I am grateful today for the details of my life.
Today I am strong and healthy.

Take time now to write the personal affirmations that come to mind in the space provided below:

Chapter 4

How We Communicate

"Communication is to relationships what breath is to life."

—Virginia Satir

As I began to stretch toward my potential, dealing with the changes both I and the universe had created, my younger brother, Richard, and his wife were anticipating their first child. To celebrate Hannah's arrival, they asked me to be with them at her birth. They knew I was struggling over being childless and wanted me to be able to bond with my niece. As I walked into the hospital that day, I was filled with conflicting emotions, and not at all sure how I was going to respond to this life-altering event. But the birth of this new life was an unbelievable and deeply moving experience. I was filled with joy as I saw her body awaken into life. And then, just minutes after her arrival, my brother called out her name. *"Hannah, Hannah,"* he said softly, and she turned her head as she seemed to remember that sound from the deep watery world of the unborn.

After welcoming Hannah and watching her blue eyes close for a well-deserved rest after her journey into the world, Richard and I went back to his house. As soon as I sat down, I started crying. I cried all afternoon and into the evening. He was completely understanding and comforted me with brotherly hugs. It broke my heart that I couldn't take Hannah home with me. My inner voice felt helpless, and longed to have a child of my own to love. I was passively dealing with the challenges in my life from a victim stance, without a solution, rather than using my outer voice to ask for what I wanted. Based on my limited exposure to the world of ideas and solutions, I had predetermined that there was no resolution.

Later, when I'd finally run out of tears, Richard gently suggested that I hadn't asked the universe or my husband, Arthur, for my heart's desire. I told him we had talked about it and that Arthur didn't really want to adopt, so I felt I had no chance of ever having a child. Richard had just attended a personal growth seminar, and told me I hadn't *really* asked. "Why don't you call Arthur right now," he said, "and I'll sit here with you while you *really* ask."

Through a new torrent of tears, I explained to Arthur that I'd witnessed Hannah's birth and I knew *beyond any doubt* that I wanted a child more than anything in the world.

There was a long pause, and then he said, "Okay, let's talk about it when you get home." I conveyed his words to Richard, who urged me to tell him *again*.

So I did. I said, "I want you to understand I REALLY, REALLY, REALLY *want a child!*" Then my words slipped away as I sobbed uncontrollably. I hung up and my brother comforted me.

When I got home that night, Arthur and I didn't talk much about it, and for the sake of peace in our household, I let the matter drop. And then about six months later, out of the blue, Arthur told me that in spite of his silence, he'd been thinking a lot about my need to have a child. He told me that he'd made an appointment with an agency that worked with surrogate mothers. I was as ecstatic as I was shocked. I threw my arms around him. "You really did hear me!" I could hardly believe that I was going to have a chance to raise a child.

Today I have a beautiful daughter, a gift from my

husband, my brother, the universe, an unusual agency and a very special woman named Carol. To communicate assertively for what we truly desire in life empowers us in ways we do not even realize.

Communication and the Path of Change

The Fearless Change Map shows us that our treasure, the fulfillment of our needs, listed on the upper-left side of the Map, is interdependent on our ability to communicate with a person, a place or the energy of creation. Being interdependent means we need to take care of ourselves through both independent and dependent actions. In some situations we need to postpone pursuing our basic needs because of more pressing events, so we avoid our exercise, eat snacks instead of meals and stay up too late. What creates problems is when we ignore taking care of ourselves, or we can't or won't risk asking because we fear the need will never be met and we'll be criticized or become too vulnerable.

As explained in the previous chapter, our beliefs about the fulfillment of needs determine whether we feel trust or whether we're limited by fear as change approaches. When our words and intentions are clear, we know our boundaries and how to protect ourselves in a healthy way. When we are in alignment with our needs our body language is congruent as we ask the universe for assistance. Often the solution we envision is shortsighted, whereas the universe's answer may be different but more fulfilling. How we handle this depends on our ability to feel safe.

During the years when I was extremely independent, I didn't trust others to do anything for me, nor was I able to set boundaries or feel safe in an intimate relationship. Instead, I found people to take care of to increase my sense of control over my own life. Without an assertive voice I was unequipped to let others know what worked or didn't work for me.

On the other hand, when I thought that I didn't have to take responsibility for my emotional or financial well-being, then I was dependent, because I'd sacrificed my voice and my personal power. We can't draw boundaries if we haven't defined the perimeters of who we are in a relationship. Being *inter*dependent is that beautiful mix of both; realizing that we need others' ideas, support and companionship and that we need to develop our self-reliance by doing things on our own.

We learn how—or how not—to communicate in our encounters with our families, friends and our community. Through awareness of these interactions we gain understanding about our world and ourselves.

As we talk about the change and loss we're experiencing, we release the past and unveil possibilities of new beginnings. Some changes are easy to talk about. Others can bring up shame, doubt and vulnerability. Change can reveal aspects of ourselves and others that we were unaware of, or it can rekindle unresolved issues. Memories of loss of love and safety, as experienced through trauma, death, divorce and illness, may surface as anger, anxiety, bouts of tearfulness or avoidance. These are signs to us that in the past our needs were not met. Fulfillment and nurturance in the present help to soothe and heal both past and current wounds.

Passive Communication

Look at the Path of Fear on the far left-hand side of the Fearless Change Map (page 6) and follow the arrows down.

Often we tend to try to inwardly control a situation rather than acknowledge the signs of change. We then feel hurt if our needs aren't being met, even though we haven't expressed them to others. Being more inward, our reaction on this side is to have self-control. We isolate, feel guilty and become depressed, all of which can lead to illness or addiction. And in the midst of all our pain, we're often unaware that there is change going on.

Sara, one of my clients, demonstrates her passivity by pulling away physically and not saying much. She listens quietly, her voice is soft, and there is shyness about her. No one pays much attention to her and she can slip in and out of situations as if she were nearly invisible. She wears beige most of the time, her camouflage color. She has difficulty getting her needs met because she's not trusting or confident enough to ask others to help her fulfill them. And she's not sure she's worthy of being fulfilled. Sara has internalized her resentments by oversleeping and blocking her creativity, the ultimate source of her solution.

As we release the barriers to our emotions and pay attention to our feelings, we discover creative solutions to life's challenges. Before I learned how to be assertive and began defining what healing would look and feel like, I, too, had a difficult time expressing my needs. I couldn't really understand what others said, so I would just sit there and put on my nice-girl smile. I could be passive or aggressive, but not direct and assertive. I was overwhelmed. I took on more projects than I could handle, and failed to grasp the limitations of time and energy. I thought that if I *thought* I could do it, then I *should* be able to complete the project. When we're undergoing change, doing something brand new, how do we know how far we can stretch? Time and experience, plus an assertive voice to maintain our boundaries and inner balance, will provide the answer.

Aggressive Communication

The other spectrum on the Path of Fear is aggressive expression. It's shown in red on the left side of the Fearless Change Map. When responsibility for our own potential, our self-actualization, is avoided and projected through blame and manipulation of others to live that aspect of us which we are denying, we often feel stressed and become controlling. We may even assume responsibility for others but not really listen to what they're saying. Or we become self-centered, wanting the world to respond to our perspectives and expectations. Randy, a client of mine who grew up as the eldest of seven children in a single-parent household, would complain about his wife's lack of interest in sporting activities to deal with her weight issues. Yet when asked to give his own exercise schedule, he admitted that he didn't do any physical exercise himself. Randy believed he was responsible for telling her how to stay healthy because he felt he always had to have the answers.

Many of us were raised in homes where there was addiction or illness, and we began taking on adult responsibilities even as children. We were robbed of a normal childhood where we could learn to balance work and play. Instead, we grew up with the belief that we were responsible for everyone and everything. As adults, we may be angry because we still feel responsible if life doesn't go according to our childhood expectations, which provided order in an otherwise chaotic arena. We may have been denied the developmental process of detachment, and enjoyment of life. We may not know how to relinquish control, and fear that if we "let go," we'll lose all our strength and power. When we're constantly angry and aggressive, we tend to get into squabbles when someone else's view differs from ours. So we do what we know best: We try to "fix" them to think like us, by imposing our beliefs and values. Aggressive communication is marked by words or intent that is forceful, manipulative, sarcastic or even explosive.

I have another client named Helen, who, when being aggressive, interrupts others to express her displeasure. She doesn't listen well, and projects her voice as she tries to take control. Her facial expressions aren't pretty either; she glares and assumes a "*Go ahead, make my day*" pose. Helen doesn't ask that her needs be met, she *demands*. As you can imagine, she often hurts people's feelings, or gets into power struggles. She creates more problems rather than moving toward a solution. Helen's cycles of fear-driven behavior continued until she finally got the message that her behavior was upsetting others. Through an intervention at work she was referred to counseling and learned to become aware of her interactions with her co-workers. Now, if she finds herself being aggressive, she asks two important questions: What do I need right now? What did I take from that person?

As her awareness increased, Helen began to see things differently. By reframing our thoughts about a situation, we can reprogram our response so that it's more empowering for everyone.

Passive-Aggressive Communication

Being passive-aggressive doesn't solve the problem either. When my client, Tom, was being passive-aggressive, his body language and voice were passive, but under the surface he was angry because his needs were not being met. The problem was that he wasn't articulating them well enough to get results. His anger was too uncomfortable to own, so Tom consciously or unconsciously repressed it and tended to avoid things his wife or his boss asked him to do. His anger then seeped out, and they responded by getting upset with him, blaming others or internalizing their own anger. Tom's wife developed a chronic health condition due to the frustration of trying to get Tom to be a willing and supportive partner. Because of her own unmet needs, she became sarcastic and critical, and tried to guilt-trip Tom into teamwork. As a couple they developed a depressed family system, wherein no one felt truly empowered.

Sometimes in our relationships we tend to make change by altering our roles. The formerly passive person becomes aggressive, or vice versa, and the dynamics within the relationship switch corners. But no real change occurs. Neither a passive nor an aggressive voice will fulfill our needs for self-respect, personal responsibility, friendship, inner peace, love or belonging.

Assertive Communication

Review the Path of Trust on the right-hand side of the Fearless Change Map (page 6). Follow the arrows down. When we accept our reality, we use an assertive voice, cooperate with the environment and with ourselves. There isn't much internal conflict, as our needs, values and behavior are in alignment with the source of our fulfillment. We identify what we need, then negotiate it, and play fairly with others. We take the actions necessary to care for ourselves, and are open to creative solutions. As we do, we feel increasingly empowered and satisfied, and growth is assured.

Another client, Barbara, claimed her assertive voice as a result of leaving a verbally abusive relationship. After a lifetime of being passive, she began to ask for what she wanted and believed that she deserved. Throughout the course of our work together, she found her confidence, learned to make direct eye contact, and her previously fragile voice became clear and strong. Her family and friends couldn't believe how she had blossomed. Barbara now believes she is supposed to be here, doing whatever she's doing. She easily makes "I" statements and takes responsibility for her thoughts and actions. When she feels uncertain, she writes out a script, practices it in the mirror or with one of her friends until she's confident enough to take action. If she's concerned about the other person's response, she has her friend role-play with her. Then, just like political candidates preparing for televised debates, Barbara keeps rehearsing until she comes up with responses that will empower her. When she's assertive in her communication, she moves into the solution and feels good about the outcome. Barbara has now established mental and verbal boundaries within her own psyche and knows how to set comfortable limits.

Once in a while even the use of assertive words, strong eye contact, a calm voice and a well-stated request does not bring us what we want or need. (Even ultimate winners sometimes lose debates.) But we always feel better for stating the truth. To be assertive in some families may provoke someone else's aggression because you've broken the family code of silence. By not talking about what's going on, we're resisting the natural flow of change and growth. When trauma or abuse has occurred in our lives, talking about it soon afterward is the best way to begin healing. The longer we hold off talking about what really happened, the more negative the impact on everyone, as the family system adapts to unspoken emotional pain.

Our personality patterns that are genetically and spiritually based, as well as learned communication styles, determine how we perceive the world and express our feelings and words. On some issues, we're optimistic and hopeful, sharing our enthusiasm and motivating others to reach to the next level of healing and growth. With other issues, such as violence, sexual or physical abuse, either by us or toward us, we lose our motivation to speak assertively. We may act passively and try to avoid confrontations, and withdraw to what we think is a position of safety. We want to believe that if we don't look at the issue closely, it will go away and we won't have to say or do anything to reclaim our sense of true personal power. We may even believe that the task we ultimately face will be so overwhelming that it will destroy us or that we will destroy another. We may think it might be easier for someone else to talk about *it*, so we don't have to face our fears. Yet in spite of our resistance, facing *it*, talking about *it* and taking back our power is exactly what we must do. Others of us aggressively confront our problems by venting our frustration through blame, intimidation and toxic words to show our power. Aggression is a false power and because it leaves one feeling empty, with no real change, it only leads to more aggressive acts. When we use our assertive voice, we'll survive and thrive as we move through life's changes.

Healing the Past

The authentic communication necessary to resolve family and relationship problems is often blocked and distorted because we don't have the skills to communicate assertively. Childhood abuse and betrayal hinders the development of our boundaries and our ability to say no. Many children are not allowed to express their hurt feelings or their needs for love, attention and personal power. Instead, these issues surface only during arguments and power struggles. It's easy to get stuck in the problem, communicating either consciously or unconsciously that there are no solutions. This chronic feeling of confusion fosters feelings of helplessness and depression. When we internalize that sense of impotence, we experience withdrawal and passive communication. When these emotions are acted outward, in an aggressive manner, helplessness manifests as yelling, irritability, frustration, and verbal or physical abuse.

Abuse — which became a household word during the O.J. trials — is an epidemic. It is an expression of anger and a sense of temporary power. Abuse is expressed through physical and emotional neglect, and through verbal, physical, sexual, spiritual and religious control. Because outbursts of anger don't really change the dynamics or eliminate feelings of helplessness, people begin to rationalize its acceptability, and trust is soon replaced by feelings of betrayal and a lowered sense of esteem and worth. When we can no longer connect with our families, we jeopardize our emotional and spiritual wellness unless we open ourselves to healing. The trauma of betrayal scars relationships, and spills over into our workplaces and neighborhoods, generation after generation until there is change. Family members are pitted against one another in retaliation for their inability to identify needs and effectively ask to have them met. The trust that's needed for healthy growth gets buried as fear becomes dominant.

We heal when we can tell others about past or present hurts, and thus allow them to witness our experience. Sometimes we can end abuse in the present moment by simply removing ourselves from the situation. As we take an empowering action we increase our self-esteem and open ourselves to a new level of conscious awareness. As we become aware of our limits and can articulate them, we avoid re-abusing ourselves through self-sacrifice. When we're no longer willing to tolerate mistreatment — either by our own hand or that of others, we discover our self-respect.

Some of us choose to confront those who have hurt us. Others find comfort in the support of those who have experienced similar events. By identifying how you feel, and telling another person, you set an important boundary that will continue to give you strength as you move through the changes in your life. Telling your truth reconnects you with your personal power.

As we begin to identify and heal the resentments toward those who have inflicted pain, we need to forgive. If we're afraid to forgive, or fear that forgiveness is condoning bad behavior, we end up being imprisoned by our resentment. My friend, Sherry, who stays well through her ability to accept and forgive others, says that "Resentment is the poison you swallow and expect someone else to get sick." When we realize that our resentments don't punish others, but only hurt us, we can start to take responsibility for our spiritual growth. When we truly forgive, we experience emotional and spiritual healing.

Establishing New Boundaries

As we desire healing and open ourselves to accept life as it is, we set the stage for redefining our boundaries and drawing opportunities and experiences that nurture us through our change. We say "yes" to these new paths of light and creativity. With boundaries, I'm able to tell others how their behavior affects me, I can leave an unpleasant situation and not feel guilty; I don't have to "fix" anyone; and no one can make me feel wronged. I don't have to stay in a job or relationship because I think I *should*. I stay because I *choose* to. I feel trust in myself, and my ability to steer my life on a positive path and through the changes ahead. When I have these invisible fences in place, I know what I need and how much I can do, eat or say, for example, without becoming overwhelmed or overwhelming someone else. If I do get swamped with commitments, I know it's not etched in stone. It's okay to be flexible, say "no" or "I'm going to need more time with this."

If we're able to identify the inner experience of being tired, hungry or in need of positive connection, we can successfully rebalance our inner and outer needs and priorities during times of change. Melinda used to pick arguments with her husband, Phil, quite regularly until one night after attending a Fearless Change workshop she realized that all she really wanted was a nice big hug to feel reconnected to him.

Over the years I made many choices that weren't in my best interests because I didn't have the ability to identify what I really needed, or say a simple "no," or negotiate what I did or didn't want. I felt pretty helpless because I wasn't able to articulate the specific aspects of the job or relationship that were unfulfilling.

So I did what lots of people do, I *went along to get along*. The problem with this approach is that one day I woke up and realized I'd compromised myself because I didn't say what I really wanted. Then I was angry because I hadn't been true to myself. Saying "yes" because we were never taught that it's okay to say "no" causes a lot of heartache for everyone.

The following are a few of the problems I've encountered as a result of not being able to say "no," set boundaries or use my assertive voice.

Problems I Had When I Didn't
Use My Assertive Voice

1. Dated when I would have been better off doing what I wanted to do in the first place: stay home and do my hair.
2. Didn't keep my commitment to myself to study for classes I was taking.
3. Made poor relationship decisions.
4. Bought a house I didn't like.
5. Lied about my feelings toward the person I was dating because I couldn't say, "I like you only as a friend."
6. Ignored signs from my body that the party, the job or the date wouldn't be safe.
7. Took on too much responsibility in a volunteer position, then didn't know how to say I couldn't do it all.

Through claiming an assertive voice, we can change our beliefs about relationships, experience honesty and respect. We talk about the *past* to discover what we'd like to do differently *now*, to carry forward to the *future*. When we each take responsibility for our part in an upset or poor communication, and establish healthy assertive dialogue, we re-create our relationships.

Solutions I Experienced As a Result of Using My Assertive Voice

1. Said I wanted out of a relationship with a man that didn't nurture me and refused to go back.
2. Told a man who harassed me to stop and he did. I felt empowered.
3. Found inspiration by opening my Bible and discovering the passage in Matt 7:7, "Ask and it shall be given you; seek and you shall find; know and it shall be opened unto you."
4. Prepared myself through education and training to apply or a job I dreamed of having and was given the position.
5. Applied for financial aid and grants to get my education.
6. Let people help me along my spiritual journey through asking for help and guidance.
7. I am able to ask for help and still feel strong.

As we acknowledge our interdependence on others, we come to know our strengths and limitations and learn how and when to ask for assistance. Embrace the choices of Fearless Change, practice being assertive with yourself and others, and you'll start to make decisions to construct this new reality for yourself. Once you ask for what you want and don't want, you'll have shown self-respect and modeled how to set appropriate boundaries. Actions speak louder than words. ⊱

Chapter 5

Identifying Our Needs

"All things for which you pray and ask, believe that you have received them, and they shall be granted you."

— Mark 11:24

To know that we can satisfy our basic needs promotes self-esteem, good health and joy. Fulfilling the details of our lives is what we require as humans to function and maintain our physical, emotional and spiritual health. Our need for love, respect, safety, and honesty are as nonnegotiable as our need for food, water and shelter. Yet, from the beginning of civilization, nearly all families have been marked by the trauma of war and natural disasters. Famine, poverty, ignorance, abuse, secrets, mental illness and addiction evolve from the destruction. Millions of people each day are unable to meet their own basic needs, let alone those of their children. My family was no exception.

After surviving World War II, my father, like so many veterans, returned with a level of stress and trauma that affected every aspect of his life. Being patient and attending to the needs of four children was not easy for him. As a result I felt guilty for having needs, guilty for *wanting*.

I was taught that there are no real necessities beyond food, water, shelter and clothing. I was shamed as a child for needing attention and guidance. As in many families during that period of time, displays of affection were withheld. I learned early on to disown my need for things like self-esteem, emotional trust and spiritual connection, since they weren't part of our family structure. Like most families, the goal was to teach us to be self-reliant. There were demands and expectations about how we spent our time in the pursuit of survival. "Work hard, study and achieve" were the messages. The dread of being dependent was countered by my family's emphasis on independence, rather than finding the balance of being *inter*dependent. It seemed that no matter what I asked for, whether it be help with homework, a hand with reaching a glass on the top shelf, or just the comfort of a good-night kiss, my pleas were met with intimidating words and behaviors. No matter how I framed my words, my interactions with my dad would set him off and he would become angry and critical. I wasn't enough, nor could I *do* enough of the right things to quiet his harsh and critical voice.

I began to compensate for my unmet needs by seeking approval from others. In time I became a perfectionist. When I was about ten, I started sewing my own clothes, using money I earned from pulling weeds and selling homemade corsages. I would scream and throw a tantrum if the clothes or flowers weren't perfect, then wonder why I still felt empty.

My mother and role model later confided that she had denied her own needs to the point that she was unable to give to herself. So, like her, I learned to protect myself by keeping my needs down to the bare-bones minimum. As a result I often denied even hunger, thirst and pain. I didn't want to bother anyone or be criticized for asking, so I became sort of a cross between Joan of Arc and a warrior princess.

A serious back problem, the result of a birth defect in my lower spine and minor case of polio, went undiagnosed until my aunt noticed that I was limping and my spine had grown crooked.

This disability created multiple changes and losses in my life as I exchanged my dancing, music and sports activities for the rigors of physical therapy, surgeries, casts and braces. My problems created a domino-like-effect that rippled through our family, imposing on everyone's time, space, relationships and resources. Years later I realized that we were not unlike the majority of families throughout the world who struggle to raise children and keep a roof over their heads.

My need to be perfect intensified as I felt the shame of my body's distortion. It was hard to accept that my back would never regain its prior strength and flexibility, and I hadn't yet realized that my limitations would affect my choices for the rest of my life. I could not unconditionally accept who I was. I desperately needed approval from others to learn how to give it to myself.

As an adult, I became a perfectionist. My home was spotless on the off chance that someone might drop in. I was sure they'd reward my efforts by exclaiming, "Judy keeps such a clean house!" It was hard on my already damaged back to push myself, but I believed that napping in the middle of the day was unacceptable (never mind that President John F. Kennedy and other notables indulged), so I kept slaving away. And I continued to aggravate my back and then self-medicate, always denying my body's need for care.

Deprivation had become a twisted source of personal power, the power of sacrifice. I became a champion of the *If I don't ask for anything then you can't criticize or reject me* mentality.

My addiction took hold through pain medication, tranquilizers and alcohol. I then overcompensated and tried to fulfill myself externally. Filling myself up from the outside in, I created unhealthy dependencies. As the Fearless Change Map shows us, when we try to control ourselves, we bury our trauma and pain, ignore our body's cry for help and feel helpless. To shut down our bodies to better deny our needs, as in the case of addictions or eating disorders, we develop a form of passive control and self-destructive behavior. If we stifle ourselves, we feel disconnected to the prosperity in our world.

Before I knew what I needed, I denied myself any kind of emotional nurturing. Jumping the hurdles in life is easier when we can feel our emotions and ask, "Do I need to feel more trust, love, belonging, intellectual growth, creative expression, rest or renewal? What would help me to feel stronger and calmer?" The first step in that direction is to recognize what your body is telling you. Taking care of ourselves has to be the first priority.

Over the years I have put together a list of needs, which I review regularly. Those that are unmet I see as goals, and I use affirmations and visual images to draw them to me. Today I have more physical stamina, manage my time better, feel closer to my spirit and my relationships are more intimate. And always, I do whatever I can to avoid physical, emotional or spiritual hunger.

Identifying Your Needs

During a major change, our schedules shift and priorities get out of sync. The pressures of raising a family, climbing the corporate ladder or healing from an injury or illness can throw us off balance. Abraham Maslow, a noted humanistic psychologist, realized that getting our needs met was the basis of wellness. As he studied hundreds of people who'd been successful in handling change, he created categories of these requirements and a hierarchy in which they were fulfilled, with the primary needs first, and the growth needs emerging from the basis of our inner and outer strength.

Basic Needs

1. Physical safety and sustenance

2. Love and belonging

Growth Needs

3. Esteem through self-respect

4. Esteem through respect from others

5. Understanding and knowledge

6. Aesthetics

7. Self-actualization

Each of these categories is composed of several different needs that are necessary if we are to thrive. I've added some needs to his list, which I believe are essential for building a solid foundation. I call them *The Foundational Fifty*!

Take a minute to identify a need you have today and be willing to do whatever it takes to get it fulfilled. Be willing to challenge the beliefs you learned from your family and prior experiences. Practice being assertive and making "I" statements, such as "I need_____." Making healthy changes doesn't take a lot of time, it just takes willingness to move beyond the uncomfortable feelings and rationalizations established by years of negative thinking and actions.

Needs Required for
Basic Survival

PHYSICAL	SAFETY	TO LOVE & BELONG
Oxygen Sleep and rest Food and drink Exercise and recreation Environmental comfort Emotional release Sexual expression Spiritual connection Solitude	Safe from harm Emotional trust Financial security Prosperity Vocational expression Consistency Routine Fairness Security and stability	Love self Love others Feel loved Belong in our families Belong in our communities Understand others Understood by others Share common interests Care for others

Needs Required for
Growth

ESTEEM OURSELVES	ESTEEM THROUGH OTHERS	TO KNOW & UNDERSTAND	SEEK BEAUTY	SELF ACTUALIZE
Self-esteem Tell the truth Self-respect Competence Adequacy Achievement Mastery	Desire for acceptance Respect from others Hear the truth Recognition Reputation Appreciation Status Prestige	Satisfy curiosity Explore Discover Find solutions Relationship meaning Intellectual challenge	Enjoy beauty and art	Utilize potential to become self-fulfilled

Adapted from the Hierarchy of Needs — Abraham Maslow, Ph.D.

Over the years of working with others, I've noticed that most relationship problems occur because people don't take the time, energy or responsibility for meeting their own needs. They instead expect that their partner, employer, child, friend or society should make them feel whole. When we take the time and introspection to identify and assume responsibility for satisfying our needs, we establish high self-esteem and self-actualization.

The next section, "Filling Up Our Empty Cups", describes many of these human needs. At the beginning of each, you'll find a chart that will help you identify what it feels like to have a particular need fulfilled — or unfulfilled--along with suggestions for meeting these needs. The *Foundational Fifty*, a guidebook available from Lasting Recovery Publications, includes a complete assessment of your basic and growth needs to help you determine which ones are unmet *for you*, right now. The guidebook explores all fifty needs in depth, along with insightful questions and a format to help you establish a workable plan. You'll see how some of these needs have been satisfied throughout your life, and how others remain unfulfilled.

FILLING UP OUR EMPTY CUPS

Basic Needs

As children, our basic needs for food, shelter and safety may or may not have been met either by our parents, extended family or community. As we mature into young adulthood and leave our known structure, it becomes *our* task to acquire food and shelter, friends, work and a means of reaching our potential. We usually do this by trial and error, which means taking risks and finding our faith. Once basic physical needs have been secured we can begin fulfilling our needs for love and belonging. We earn our place in a group by being truthful, caring about others and sharing common interests. We seek esteem though self-respect and respect from others. We gain further confidence by learning to love ourselves and pursue self-confidence through achievement and mastery. Once we've acquired work and found a place in our community, we not only want a paycheck and a stable organization, we want acceptance and recognition from others, and more knowledge and understanding of how things work. To satisfy our intellectual curiosity, we read books, take classes and embark on new projects. All the while we're beginning to appreciate the beauty in our world, as we evolve into the final stage of development—self-actualization, the full development of who we are.

But even when we "have it made," the spirit of change shows itself through a job change, a divorce, move or health-related problem. This shift requires us to alter our priorities, as our attention focuses again on the earlier physiological and safety needs. Even the most supportive network is constantly shifting and we must go back to our basic needs to reclaim the center of our strength and make the changes in our priorities to gain our inner and outer balance.

In turbulent times we tend to neglect our exercise routines and healthy diets, put off calling family and friends, and sometimes we forget to pay bills. Some of us worry that our feelings of self-esteem, belonging or understanding will never return. We wonder what went wrong until we figure out how to see what's right in the situation and begin looking for the "gift."

It's best to first get clear on the specifics of change and how it affects other areas of our life. Has our support system changed because of a death or addiction in our life—or in the life of someone close to us? Do we expect other people or things to fulfill us and in turn fail to listen to our bodies? Have our close friends or relatives moved away? Has an injury or illness caused us to give up our gym workouts or favorite sport? Has a job change placed us among strangers? When we relocate—either by choice or chance—both our inner and outer environments are in temporary turmoil. (This has been known to happen even during home remodeling.) Our sleeping, eating, exercise and other basic daily needs are disturbed. If we've moved to a different part of the country, not only do we have to seek out new supermarkets and schools, but we may need to adjust to new weather and cultural climates. In the case of a romantic or marital breakup, relationships with in-laws or mutual friends may become strained or even severed. Here is where we utilize the choices of Fearless Change to reframe and reinvent our lives. These choices support us in continuing to make wise choices that will get us back on track. By letting go of the *way it was*, exploring new options, visualizing the future and staying positive, we will move forward again into lightness and growth. Life is a process, so readjustment may take time, energy, money and patience, yet most people find that the old axiom is true: When one door closes, another will open.

In my own life, I spent a couple of years trying to figure out which career path would awaken my passion. Reading an article on goals, I discovered that I needed to be needed. With most of my family gone, and my friends involved with their own lives, and unable to have children, I didn't feel needed—by anybody. One day when our city was rocked by a minor earthquake, I realized that in a major catastrophe, I wouldn't be *first* on anybody's call list. But with the realization that I needed to feel needed, I knew I'd discovered gold. I then asked my spirit to guide me into experiences that would fulfill this need. I have felt fulfilled ever since, and take responsibility to make my space interesting, enjoyable and valuable to me.

1. Physiological and Safety Needs

When we care for our physical well-being, we strengthen the foundation for our attitude, our perceptions, and the intention of what we communicate to others and ourselves, minute by minute. Included in these needs are oxygen, sleep and rest, food, exercise, shelter, emotional and sexual release, and spiritual connection. Safety needs protect us from harm by setting our inner and outer boundaries. These needs include emotional trust, consistency, fairness, routine, stability and security. It's natural to become frightened at times during the process of change, until we have more information, but fulfilling these needs benefits us in many areas as we rebuild.

To meet her need for exercise, Joanna arranged to join her neighbor every morning for a 30-minute walk before getting the kids up for school. Sam and Helen joined a gym and even through they had different workout schedules, they were both making the effort to strengthen their bodies and minds. When Sam injured his knee at work and couldn't exercise for three months, Helen kept on with her routine. The last time I saw them, Sam was a bit down because he couldn't return to his vigorous workouts of the past, but he was signing up for a yoga class so he could maintain his solution-oriented mindset while keeping his body strong and flexible.

Sleep and Rest

Unfulfilled	Satisfied	Try This:
We have difficulty falling or staying asleep, or wake up too early; we sleep too much or maintain an erratic schedule becoming irritable and tired.	We feel rested, sleep deeply, maintain a regular sleep schedule; we feel energized throughout the day, are able to rest when necessary.	♥ Wake up at the same time each day. ♥ Learn progressive muscle relaxation techniques and do them before going to sleep. ♥ Develop a sleep routine. ♥ Light a fragrant candle or drink chamomile tea before retiring; write in your journal.

It's not always easy to get a good night's sleep. We lie awake at night because of pain, indigestion, excitement, worry, hunger or nightmares. Getting to sleep is easiest when we can clear our mind by writing down the thoughts that clamor for our attention. Lana had difficulty sleeping and would stay awake at night trying to decide what to do about her relationship. She would be so tired the next day that she'd often need a nap after she got home from work, then she'd lie awake at night again. Her co-workers complained that she was irritable, and she began to eat high-calorie snacks in an attempt to boost her energy. Her sleep cycle was thrown off until she made a practice of going to bed and getting up at a regular time.

Lana allowed herself 20 minutes at bedtime to write out all the things that were on her mind, then she listened to a meditation tape and learned progressive muscle relaxation techniques to quiet her mind and body. As Lana became more aware of the process of letting go of the day and transitioning into sleep, she felt more rested, happier, and was able to enjoy life again. Our overall physical and emotional health improves as we take a time-out to regenerate and allow ourselves permission to rest.

Emotional Release

UNFULFILLED	SATISFIED	TRY THIS:
We feel tense, tired, over-whelmed, and want some form of escape.	We discover healthy release of our feelings and reclaim our sense of personal power.	♥ Keep a journal of your emotions. ♥ Smash aluminum cans. ♥ Work in your garden. ♥ Discover a safe way to express your feelings as they surface.

Take the necessary moments to nurture your emotions during times of change. Spend time alone and allow yourself to feel your sadness, fear, relief, anxiety and excitement. These often complex emotions are indicators that movement and growth is necessary, much like a bud emerging on a vine. Emotional release is our ability to surrender to the expressions of loss, or personal powerlessness over a person, place or situation, and the realization that we must move on in our lives. In the safe arena provided by a supportive friend or professional, we can begin to shed the armor that has both protected us and blocked our growth.

As we play, make love, cry, listen to music, work on a project, build something, play a musical instrument, create art, write, sculpt or get a massage, we release our emotions. When we're emotionally open during a transition, we're able to let go of the past and find our voice to fulfill our most important needs.

How? Allow yourself to cry when you are sad. Tears cleanse your body. Shout out your angst to the world when you're upset (preferably in a secluded place), as it will help you reclaim your energy and clarity. Try new ways of expressing your emotions, in safe ways, without attacking others. Work in the garden, sing a song, write a poem, build a shelf, throw a Frisbee, take a walk or listen to a comedy tape. Do whatever it takes to refresh yourself and clear your soul.

Emotional release often dissolves physical pain that's been blocked by unresolved issues. Take a minute now and mentally scan your body for tension. Our bodies respond to what we say and feel. Louise Hay, minister, author and healer, says that all pain and illness is the result of hanging on to resentments and thereby blocking the natural flow of love. My personal and professional experience reveals the same truth. Focus on forgiveness to release the fears and hurts. Awaken to your relationship with God, your inner healer. Find a quiet time to write in your journal or compose a letter to say *good-bye, I miss you, I forgive you* or *I love you*. Relax and let go.

Spiritual Connection

UNFULFILLED	SATISFIED	TRY THIS:
We feel irritable, resistant, unproductive, overwhelmed, physically tense, disconnected.	We feel our inner strength, receive insight and guidance to make decisions and flow with life; we feel relaxed and connected to our deeper self.	♥ Pray and let go. ♥ Meditate at the same time each day. ♥ Sit quietly for three minutes, journal for 10minutes. ♥ Practice silence; listen rather than speak today.

Spiritual needs are those feelings of connection to our real selves that provide meaning and purpose. Our bond with spirit is the foundation of Fearless Change. When we listen to our inner thoughts and honor our intuition and inspirations, we are assured that we're on our right path. We can trust that we'll be shown everything we need to manifest our healing.

Spiritual fulfillment can be found through unconditionally loving others, or by reveling in nature's colors, textures, smells and essence. Take a minute during your next walk and just stop and look around. Remember as a child how you stopped and smelled the flowers? Perhaps you even picked a daisy for your mom or a special friend. Be childlike today and flop down on the ground, caress the flowers, climb a tree and take time for some deep cleansing breaths as you inhale nature's fragrances. Conscious deep breathing, especially in a peaceful setting, increases our awareness of the spirit.

This natural longing for internal spiritual connection is often misinterpreted as a need for something external. We may feel the hunger for spirit though our sense of deprivation. Spiritual deprivation comes from ignoring the inner bond with our self, and often originates in childhood when we had to disregard our spiritual core. This happens when we're neglected or treated badly by the adults in our lives.

When I was young, my mother told me not to keep a journal because someone might read it, so I avoided writing about my feelings until years later when I began my healing journey. For years I only wrote academic papers because I didn't think my personal revelations were valuable, and I also feared they might be used against me.

Before I started writing this book, I was creatively frustrated, and every time I'd sit down in the living room, I would get the urge to redecorate or knock out a wall. (What a nightmare that would have been!) As I began the writing process, I reconnected to an even deeper place within myself and found, to my relief, that I no longer need to reshuffle my environment.

To fulfill herself spiritually, Lorene made a spiritual connection in her 12-step group, and to her surprise, she also reconnected with a friend she hadn't seen since high school. David returned to his childhood church and discovered a satisfying prayer of forgiveness that provides daily comfort. Once we take the leap of faith into the void of the new, we become aware of synchronistic events, answered prayers, and the power of forgiveness. We realize they are all acts of the fulfillment and spiritual grace. When I feel anxious and not sure what I need, I pray or meditate and am soon enlightened. Listen now to the needs of your inner spirit. Trust this spirit, for it is the essence of your healing.

Safe from Harm

UNFULFILLED	SATISFIED	TRY THIS:
We're frightened of situations and relationships; we don't feel physically or emotionally safe; we avoid social situations or are too trusting of others and neglect or ignore boundaries.	We listen to our intuition and rational mind; we can use our skills to set boundaries, we recognize the safety of situations and people; we *can* take care of ourselves.	♥ Notice when you feel safe. ♥ Write down your personal boundaries. ♥ Keep your commitments to yourself. ♥ Call people you trust.

Safety needs are survival needs. I once had an office in a neighborhood where there was a known rapist, and I often worked alone late at night. Whenever I thought of the possibility of this person setting foot on my block, I pulled up my image of a brilliant white light surrounding the office building. I imagined that if this person dared violate my space, my higher power would pick him up by the scruff of the neck and haul him down to the corner where the police would be waiting. Whenever I did this, I felt safe. The rapist was soon apprehended after another therapist in the area talked him out of harming her.

The best protection we can have is an understanding of assertive communication skills. Create an image in your mind and visualize yourself saying, *I will not be treated like this again!* And mean it. Visualize the details of your experience and see yourself following through with logical consequences. Now, say it aloud, in front of the mirror. Watch your expression and keep repeating the statement until your facial expression, body language and voice tone express exactly what you mean. If I ever find myself being mistreated, I leave as soon as it's safely possible. If I'm on the street alone at night, I walk with confidence and look others in the eye so *they* know *I* know they're there. And if I encounter someone who looks threatening, I quickly visualize the best outcome in my mind's eye. When we use our mind to begin physically removing ourselves from unsafe situations, we are using our best "No" skills. These mental, verbal and emotional skills protect us from the dangerous actions of anyone who threatens our physical, emotional or financial safety.

Emotional Trust

UNFULFILLED	SATISFIED	TRY THIS:
We feel reactive and unsafe with some people and situations; we may feel panic or doubt our ability to provide for our safety.	We're more responsive to situations; we take cues from current information and give ourselves the benefit of the doubt.	♥ Listen to your body. ♥ Surround yourself with the image of white light. ♥ Practice saying "No." ♥ Notice times when you do feel safe.

To feel safe and trusting, we need a world with consistency, fairness and a sense of stability. When our environment doesn't provide these things, we react to the imbalance and develop beliefs that form and reform our view of the world.

Cindy had a history of keeping her emotions shut down. Like many of us, she knocked herself out for others as a way of avoiding her own needs and wobbly emotions. When an abusive relationship ended, Cindy finally started listening to her feelings, and began to discern how she felt around certain people. Now she's aware that when her stomach tightens up, she's feeling threatened and emotionally reactive, and when she feels secure her stomach is relaxed and she is emotionally responsive. To feel safe again, she's learning to express her emotions and her needs, and she sets firm boundaries in her relationships. By doing so she heads off potential mistreatment. To stay in a relationship where we don't feel physically and emotionally safe is self-defeating and hampers our journey into wellness. When we listen to our intuition and rational mind about people and situations, we're shown how to protect ourselves.

If people frequently mistreat us, we need to examine our beliefs about the power we extend to others. If we don't think we can survive emotionally or financially without them, then we need to examine our beliefs regarding the strength of our higher power. As we reach out to others we will learn, through trial and error, what to do. And when we make the decision to change our beliefs from fear to trust, we move forward fearlessly in our lives.

It's important to know and trust our intuition. To be in touch with our emotional intelligence means we'll be guided through the darkest of days. Cindy is actually quite intuitive about people she's not in a relationship with. Since she quit doing a *dance* to please others, and began focusing on her needs and emotions, she's honoring the intuitive voice that provides direction and guidance in her new encounters. Do you trust your emotions? Again, think about the change you're going through and write down ideas that might help you satisfy your needs for emotional trust. Remember, to heal our hearts we must first identify our needs, then, reframe our fears toward positive expectations.

2. Love and Belonging

Love

UNFULFILLED	SATISFIED	TRY THIS:
We feel unwanted, undesirable and unimportant. We sense that the flow of our daily lives passes us by.	We feel close to other people and situations, connecting through common interests, values or goals.	♥ Do something nice for someone you love. ♥ Help others less able. ♥ Be open to receive compliments and encouragement. ♥ Give someone a hug.

Love is essential to our well-being. Through our love we open the pathway to understanding others as well as ourselves. Love is the strongest healing force there is. Love brings us together, and when it's for the higher good of our soul to move on, we grow apart. When Cindy cried as she experienced her emotions and shared with her neighbor about the break-up with her boyfriend, she felt support from her formerly reclusive neighbor. Her new ally shared her story about a husband who had left her for another woman. And she later confided that until she'd felt needed by Cindy, she was unable to forgive her husband and get on with her own life. As Cindy recognized that the spirit of love was moving through her relationships, she realized she had not been loved unconditionally. Her old boyfriend had too many expectations about who he thought she *should* be. Love and concern are the basics of all satisfying relationships. Whether at home, work or in our community, we thrive on a sense of physical and emotional safety, trust, respect, understanding, caring, sharing common interests and affection. Love is expressed in a variety of ways: We see it in the smiles people give to one another, a warm handshake, a pat on the back, an encouraging word, wink, hug or validation through listening.

Family life often satisfies our intrinsic sense of belonging and love as we experience the richness of sharing holidays, camping trips, dinners and games, as well as the conflicts and challenges of daily life. We feel loved when someone listens to our problems at work, even though they may have heard them before. As we relate our struggles aloud, clarity emerges and we begin to see solutions.

On the other hand, if we've been programmed to equate love with physical and emotional abuse, we feel alone, judged and resentful, or feel disconnected from the whole of life. Many of my clients have had a difficult time believing they are loveable. Cindy learned to associate love with the universal essence of God and to visualize that energy moving through her heart into daily life.

The essence of love emanates from our higher power and is an important ingredients in our growth. The power of this unconditional love smoothes the tension of separation and guides us as we heal. We feel the presence of love through our work or churches, support groups or volunteer work. It is what brings us a sense of connection, belonging and purpose. Love, affection and a feeling of being needed allow us to contribute to our family, friends and community. Love acknowledges our worth and provides an avenue for us to give, which feels even better than receiving. Love and affection help dissolve entrenched resentments. Love and affection heal the pain in our hearts, improving our overall health and well-being.

Love can be felt through our friends, neighbors and even the strangers we encounter along our chosen path. The smile, a look of empathy or the discoveries of a common experience are all opportunities for feeling and expressing love. And it starts with loving ourselves first. Get up right now, look in the mirror, and say, "I love you,_____, unconditionally." When we love and accept ourselves first, our relationships with our children, partners and friends become easier and healthier. When we love and accept ourselves unconditionally, we pass down a legacy of respect and trust for future generations.

What we perceive in others is a mirror reflection of what we see in ourselves. When Cindy's neighbor sensed her pain, she was able to let go of her own shame and forgive herself by realizing that she wasn't alone in her suffering. If the unrealistic expectations and judgments of ourselves have been neutralized, there is only unconditional love to project onto others. When we pray for those we fear or resent, we open up to the gift of forgiveness—for us, and for them. As we shower our loving energy into the universe, we are left with feelings of compassion and kindness. We are all divine sparks coming from the same spiritual source. As we think kind thoughts, visualize and surround others with light, we increase the flow of this all-powerful love. Say a prayer for a friend, and strengthen the bond of love that connects us to the greater whole. Be kind to yourself and to others. Accept yourselves as being in the perfect place at the perfect time in the perfect way. Recognize spirit within the eyes of others.

Belonging

Unfulfilled	Satisfied	Try This:
We feel disconnected from the flow of life, doubt our abilities and worth; we're lonely, not growing toward our potential, ignoring the need to reach out to others.	We feel important, valued, secure in the knowledge that we can reach out to say hello, be a friend, perform a service or help another.	♥ Remember when felt included in the past. ♥ Call someone new. ♥ Say hello to someone in your community. ♥ Affirm aloud: *I am included in my community and family.*

A major change often upsets our sense of belonging when our transformation has to do with our work, neighborhood, relationships, friendships or families. As we separate from that which was safe and secure, we often disrupt the way we give and receive love. For each of us, and especially for our children, belonging is vital. When Margaret and her husband separated, she moved into a new apartment complex. The very next week she sent out an announcement to the other tenants that she was hosting a kids' potluck by the pool so that her children could make new friends. Several of the families came and were delighted to be able to create a sense of community for themselves and their children. No matter where we are, we belong to a community and to the human family. Remembering that *we belong* is the first step toward feeling included.

When we know we belong, we feel we have more to offer our family, team or colleagues, and we're able to accomplish more. We learn about the world through close relationships and inclusion in events, support groups and decision making at work and home. Research shows that group membership increases our physical and emotional well-being, as well as our longevity.

If you're new in a community, joining a variety of groups is the quickest way to develop a social life. When Donna realized that her new community needed a homeless shelter, she decided to support a political candidate who shared her goals. That way she could do something constructive while meeting new people. Her first assignment was the thankless job of stamping letters, but she cheerfully pitched in. Her attention to detail and high spirits soon moved her up the ladder, and she was asked to help work the door at a campaign event. It wasn't long before she was part of the team, with an ever-widening network of well-connected friends.

Find organizations that are of genuine interest and get involved in volunteer opportunities, a political campaign, the church of your choice or a professional group. And don't be discouraged if at first you strike out. You might go to a couple of luncheons or meetings and not make a connection; that's simply the law of averages. But if you persist, I can promise you that you'll make new acquaintances, and through them, meet even more people, some of whom will be kindred spirits. Friendships provide a sense of belonging and inner validation, seeing through our struggles to the humor and blessings in the challenges of change.

3. Esteem through Self-Respect

Self-Esteem

Unfulfilled	Satisfied	Try This:
We judge or criticize ourselves, creating toxic chemistry and energy within our bodies.	We're accepting and trusting of our thoughts and ideas. We trust our opinions, our intuition and act on our truth. We allow ourselves to follow our dreams, say "No" and set boundaries.	♥ Affirm aloud: *I am alive and have the right to my opinion.* ♥ Affirm aloud: *I am whole and complete. I do not need anything else to make me complete this moment.* ♥ Affirm aloud: *I forgive___.* ♥ Affirm aloud: *I am not responsible for others' actions, feelings or mistakes.*

Self-esteem is the unconditional love of self. If you hold yourself in high esteem, you're not being self-centered or narcissistic. Esteeming yourself is a form of self-approval and it's our responsibility to create this warm and loving energy for ourselves. Penny used to drift from man to man, situation to situation, always looking to others for fulfillment and approval. Problems in her relationships were beautifully healed when she began focusing on just enjoying who she is, as she allowed herself to be in the experience—right now. When we esteem ourselves, our inner light shines and we unconsciously extend that esteem to others who, in return, value us more.

Self-Respect

Unfulfilled	Satisfied	Try This:
We're unable to say "No," we over-commit, take too much responsibility for others and situations; and value the needs of others over our own needs.	We have the inner strength to solve any challenge, are able to keep our commitments for personal self-care, spiritual, intellectual and creative growth. We have high self-esteem.	♥ Practice saying "No." ♥ Take actions that honor and respect your values. ♥ Keep your commitments to yourself. ♥ Know what you need.

The boundaries of self-respect extend into the greater world. When I respect myself and forgive myself for being human, then I respect all of my experiences. I see them as they are: blessings, detours and opportunities. Sometimes we don't realize we aren't respecting ourselves. As we listen to our feelings and recognize that we can ask for what we want and need, and set comfortable limits, we start to gain that respect. When we are respectful of whom God made us to be, we stop judging ourselves and others. We must practice new thoughts if we expect others to love us without conditions or judgment.

Leo showed respect for himself when he gave up smoking. Tanya respected herself when she maintained her sexual boundaries. When Lynn's daughter spoke to her rudely, Lynn explained that her self-respect didn't permit that kind of treatment. She asked her daughter what had upset her, and when the girl confided her feelings of stress over an upcoming exam (and became aware that she was hungry), they worked out a better and non aggressive way for her to get her needs met. When we show respect for ourselves, our self-esteem grows, we stop comparing ourselves to others, we value who we are and set boundaries to honor our integrity.

Adequacy, Self-Acceptance

Unfulfilled	Satisfied	Try This:
We feel shame and have unrealistic expectations; we sacrifice our true self as we try to win approval; we make chronic comparisons, feel guilt, self-judgment, thoughts of *I should... I ought to...*	We're open to new experiences, accept mistakes as opportunities and see life as filled with choices; we experience a sense of personal power, increased self-esteem and love.	♥ Affirm aloud: *I approve of the way I handled _____.* ♥ Reframe your comparisons: *I accept myself, just as I am.* ♥ Say the Serenity Prayer each morning. ♥ Forgive yourself for your human behavior and natural limitations.

The ability to give love to one's self is a natural part of who we are, yet many of us have difficulty accepting our choices and our bodies unconditionally. I love this adapted version of the famous Serenity Prayer because when I say it, I'm reminded of the power of self-acceptance. Say this prayer right now and be aware of a difference in the way you feel about yourself and the challenge of your change:

> *God, Grant me the serenity,*
> *to accept the things I cannot change,*
> *The courage to change the things I can,*
> *and the wisdom to know the difference.*
>   *— Reinhold Neibuhr*

Say this prayer often to keep yourself grounded in the strength of truth. In the course of accepting ourselves we must choose to forgive ourselves. In doing so, we overcome our guilt for some of the choices we've made, whether it's the purchase of a God-awful outfit or an unwise love affair. Through reflection and inner stillness we come to realize that our decisions were perfect for us at the time. We can accept that we are adequate and right now we are in the perfect place at the perfect time in the perfect way, guided by the spirit of silent love. You are a loving child of this universe no matter what has transpired in your life. Moving with the current change is easier when you are giving yourself loving thoughts and gentle hugs.

4. Esteem through Respect from Others

Desire for Acceptance

UNFULFILLED	SATISFIED	TRY THIS:
We feel unwanted, undesirable, and unimportant; we sense that the flow of our daily lives passes us by.	We feel closer to other people and situations, connecting through common interests, values or goals.	♥ Ask others to talk about themselves, then: ♥ Reflect back what you heard. ♥ Do personality tests together. ♥ Be open to compliments and feedback from others.

Acceptance by others validates our sense of belonging and esteem. When we are accepted, others acknowledge their caring for us and we feel a part of something greater than ourselves. We all feel valued in our communities when we have friendly conversations, are invited to events and invite others to share our time. We are esteemed when we're accepted for our humanity. We want to be loved by our family and friends for who we have become, and for the choices we've made. Sometimes though, acceptance by those we care about is impossible due to their inability to give love, forgiveness or acceptance to themselves, or perhaps our needs are greater than what is reasonable.

Many of us seek acceptance that's unrealistic. We try to fill a need that *must* be built on a foundation of self-esteem and acceptance first. We mistakenly think that if we please others, even at the sacrifice of our own needs and wants, then we'll have our esteem validated. Cooperating with others is a step toward peace and harmony, but no one benefits when we forgo the need to cultivate our own voice, and over time we resent our sacrifices. Look to inner acceptance first, then to those in your life who *do* accept you. Remember, the universe accepts you unconditionally.

5. Understanding and Knowledge

Look for Relationships and Meaning

UNFULFILLED	SATISFIED	TRY THIS:
We feel disconnected from others, cautious in letting others know who we are; we look at the surface of things and people without interpreting the deeper message.	We find enjoyment in knowing other people and cultures; we make connections between what we think and what we perceive in our world.	♥ Notice the quality of your interactions with others. ♥ Think about the origins of your lamp, book, rock, etc. ♥ Ask someone close to you what you mean to them. ♥ Thank someone for adding meaning to your life today.

Think about your current situation, and ask yourself what it means to you. Do you interpret your job termination as an opportunity to start the business you've always dreamed about? Do you realize that the intervention at work for your drug dependence is an opportunity to see life from a new perspective? Or perhaps you've had a death in your family. Does the loss allow you to sense a new appreciation for the details of everyday life?

As we continue our exploration of life and seek deeper meaning, we listen to our intuition, become aware of synchronistic events and sense the hand of the divine in our lives.

Seek Intellectual Challenges

UNFULFILLED	SATISFIED	TRY THIS:
We believe we are too old, not smart enough or too busy to develop the potential of our mind and body.	We're open to different ideas and perspectives. We read, study and enjoy the process of learning.	♥ Learn as if there were no limitations. ♥ Get a book at the library, bookstore or go online and read about your interest. ♥ Sign up for a seminar. ♥ Talk to others about what they are learning.

Just as we seek to understand our relationships, we need to understand the systems of thought: economics, politics, religion, science and philosophy. We travel, study and yearn to know other cultures and languages. Martha was fascinated by the cultures of South America. To fulfill her need for travel and education, she gained experience as a tour guide with a local company, brushed up on her Spanish and landed a summer job with a travel group. Understanding life beyond the confines of our own community can bring us great joy. As humans we have a natural instinct to explore the unknown and to discover solutions. When we experience change in this area, we sometimes challenge our limitations, our beliefs and our finances to start new businesses or take physical or emotional risks in love and partnerships.

Intellectual needs involve curiosity, expression of our potential and the stimulation of our passions. Sometimes the mere exposure to new material can be invigorating. Whenever I've picked up one of my husband's scientific or philosophy journals, I've found a new connection with the world. When I was growing up, we spent time at the library, exploring new adventures between the covers of books. I had an aunt who had been a home economist and worked most of her life in a third-world country, teaching others. At 95 she was so excited about the latest scientific discoveries that she studied biology every day at her local library. Her love of knowledge kept her going until she was almost 100.

6. Aesthetics

Beauty in Our Surroundings

UNFULFILLED	SATISFIED	TRY THIS:
We feel empty, bored, trying to fill our inner self with superficial glamour. We value style over substance and fail to notice the true beauty that surrounds us.	We notice beauty wherever we go and enjoy the multitude of designs, colors, hues and richness of textures.	♥ Visit an art gallery. ♥ Keep a fresh flower on your table or desk. ♥ Clear out clutter. ♥ Look for the beauty all around you.

Awareness of the beauty in our surroundings brings a certain peace to our soul. Beauty awakens our own creative juices, helps us come up with new ideas and make connections between the world of thought and the world of form. Bonnie and Tom reorganized the space in their home by adding light and pleasing visuals to brighten their mood and create an essence of calm. Cindy planted a rose garden on her balcony, to symbolize the beauty of new beginnings. Start a collection of beautiful objects — shells, books, rocks, art or other items that revitalize your soul.

Many of us have blocked our creativity by giving other people or substances power over our creative lives. As we walk through the changes in our lives today, we have opportunities to awaken the sensitive side of our nature. Through meditation and prayer we become aware of creative flow through the gift of new ideas and innovative solutions. As we live out the choices of Fearless Change each day, we express our creativity through nurturing our imagination and surroundings.

7. Self-Actualization

Utilize Potential

Unfulfilled	Satisfied	Try This:
We're unsatisfied, have a sense of incompleteness about our life; we lack purpose.	We experience soul satisfaction, fulfillment of a deep desire; we have a sense of purpose.	♥ Do something creative for ten minutes today. ♥ Create affirmations as reminders. ♥ Identify what motivates you. ♥ How do you like to spend your time? Find a way to do more of it.

With our basic needs fulfilled, this time of self-actualization is for gaining mastery and utilizing our potential.

Self-actualization means realizing our visions, stretching our mind, taking risks and meeting challenges, secure in the knowledge that all is well. As we grow and develop in our vocation and our creative pursuits, we awaken our ability to see a greater overview of life. If the change you're going through is career-related, take the time to explore your options with a counselor. He or she can help you find the passion and the vocation of your soul. With the choices of Fearless Change, you can live the vision you create.

Self as Priority

We invest in ourselves when we meet our basic requirements. Even though we don't think these needs are important, or we believe that they should be met by others, we have a responsibility to do whatever we can to give and receive love, acquire a sense of belonging, and give ourselves respect and approval. The danger we face is *not putting* into place the routines that support daily exercise, good nutrition and open communication. This is the list of questions I ask myself as I contemplate the fulfillment of my needs:

1. What am I thinking in this moment?
2. Is it a fear-based or a trust-based thought?
3. What am I feeling?
4. How do I *want* to feel?
5. What do I need right now?
6. Do I believe it is available to me?
7. What am I afraid won't be there in the future?
8. What information would give me a feeling of trust?

9. How could I visualize or acquire that piece of information right now?
10. What actions can I take today toward the fulfillment of this need?

I then affirm that my need will be met. For example; *"I affirm that spirit's wonderful, new and loving friendships are all around me. I am respected, creative, and I belong."*

Allowing the Change

Change is not always comfortable. We usually have one foot in the old and one foot in the new as we demand that our higher power return us to our comfort zone. Each time there's any form of change in our lives, some of these needs are re-ordered and our priorities shift. As we define our priorities, it's essential to accept the reality of what is evolving in our lives, and understand that new priorities may provoke more intense emotions. Conscious of the fact that I *choose* my priorities, I realize that I am valuable and that I do have a sense of control over my life.

Mary, a woman I first met at a Fearless Change Workshop, came in for counseling because she was going through multiple changes in her life. She had been in recovery for about a year and a half, was divorced and had recently moved in with her parents. Mary was very scared. She'd been out of work for the past three months due to performance issues and conflict with her supervisor. She was now having difficulty with her parents' expectations and was isolated from her friends and recovery support system.

As we discussed all these changes, Mary confessed that she still missed the old days, when alcohol or pills provided an escape from her verbally abusive ex-husband. She felt that her job, like her ex-husband, had been a mismatch since day one. I helped her see that being isolated and denying her needs for connection, the loss of her chemical outlet, her husband and her job were all working against her—and endangering her recovery. Her first task was to build self-esteem. She started the Daily Self-Esteem Program she learned in the workshop. Her next task was to identify her beliefs about getting her needs met as well as to uncover her beliefs about rewarding work. I suggested she volunteer at a local recovery center to fill her days until she found a direction. While there, Mary met other women who attended meetings. A couple of them talked one afternoon about wanting to start a small business. One of them recalled the best job she'd ever had, and this reminded Mary of a temporary job she once had doing research. One of the women worked in Human Resources for a large corporation, and called Mary a few weeks later and offered her a job in the research department.

After she was hired and had put in some time in the position, Mary felt fulfilled. She was able to discover that there was a gift inherent in each of the changes she had experienced—they were seedlings to the next adventure awaiting her. Through stating what she needed, taking action to meet her requirements, and trusting the outcome, Mary gained her voice and a sense of her personal power. As her confidence grew, she understood that fear indicates the need for more information. Mary now has direction and focus for her intellectual and emotional energy, her relationships have improved, she lives on her own, and she's made many new friends. Mary reminds herself that she is on a divine path, protected and guided, and looks forward to discovering each new adventure that change brings. ≻

Part Two

"The choices of fearless change honor our
humility,
courage,
enthusiasm,
creativity,
faithfulness
and
trustworthiness."

⤙

CHOICES OF CHANGE
Embrace the Choice to
Reinvent Your Life

PROBLEM

NEW CHOICE | SOLUTION

RESIST → 1. *L*et Go | ACCEPT

DENY NEEDS → 2. *E*xplore Options | BEGIN ACTION

ISOLATE → 3. *T*alk to Others | INCLUDE YOUR NEEDS

STRESS HELPLESS VICTIM → 4. *G*row Healthy Habits | CLAIM YOUR PERSONAL POWER

ANGER DEPRESSION ILLNESS → 5. *O*pen to Growth | LOVE YOUR VISION

RAGE RELAPSE → 6. *D*iscover Benefits | BECOME FULFILLED

www.LASTINGRECOVERY.com

Chapter 6

The Choices of Change

"When we see choice instead of chance,
we become the creator of our experience."

– Alan Cohen, *Joy is My Compass*

When I make the choice to meet my needs, I accept responsibility for moving through all the changes in my life. Every day, every moment, every second I'm deciding between at least two options. I now explore the alternatives and motivate myself with uplifting thoughts and actions while imagining the best outcome possible. I commit to do what it takes and follow through with at least one action each day. Knowing I have the responsibility and the power of choice, I can grow through all my changes, both significant and minor.

There are six choices we could make each day that would bless us with peace. These choices are to Let Go, Explore our Options, Talk to Others, Create Healthy Habits, Be Open to Growth and Discover the Benefits of Change.

As you review the Choices of Change Chart on your left, you will see that all the problems symptomatic of our old behavior are based in fear. These challenges are resolved by making a viable choice. When we view our problem through the framework of the six choices, we're able to accept whatever is facing us, recommit to our developing vision and gain the strength to reinvent our life.

Each of these choices brings inherent thoughts, feelings and behaviors. We either support or deny our intellectual, emotional and spiritual growth, depending on how we choose to think and respond to each change. At the start of the phase we often find ourselves stuck in the problem, and this is where we have difficulties. We may feel anxious or grieve because we don't know how to move beyond our predicament. Or we're angry and figure that's just the way we are. Or perhaps we've given up and feel guilt, shame or hopelessness, and figure this is our lot in life. If we choose to hang on to the old because we don't believe we have a future, or we attempt to ward off the change, hoping it will go away, we become glued by our previous choices.

If, on the other hand, we trust that our needs will be met, we become assertive, direct and optimistic. Our inner voice matches our outward communication as we take action on our choices. Fearless Change incorporates ideas to help you move through turmoil until you feel empowered enough to arrive at a solution.

Embracing Choice

As you embrace change though validating your decisions, you will expand your creativity and the ability to see things in new ways. You'll then express your own view of the world to others. Making these choices will increase your self-esteem, your health and improve the intimacy and depth of your relationships with yourself, your partner and others in your world. You will be open to new ideas, opportunities and possibilities.

Be willing to explore your thoughts and feelings, and allow yourself to feel the emotions you experience along the way. Our emotions help us identify our needs. Be open to examining your underlying beliefs. Do you believe it's possible for you to meet your needs? Observe your behavior when you're feeling unfulfilled. Using your inner and outer voice, stay in the moment and affirm the fulfillment of the need. For example: *"I'm choosing to feel relaxed and confident as I explore new opportunities to meet my needs."*

As you reframe your perspective as a chance to grow and heal, it becomes so. To let go and allow the river of life to flow through you, the first choice of change is the beginning of a new and wonderful adventure. ➤

Chapter 7

Choose to Let Go

*"By letting go of the old forms, we make space
for something new to be born."*

— Eric Klein

Several years ago I made the decision to live life to the fullest, every minute of every day. I began to practice deep meditation and visualization techniques to heal a chronic pain condition. These mental exercises were also helpful in controlling anxiety as I withdrew from pain medication, then nicotine and alcohol. I meditated several times a day and visualized my body regenerating itself in this most amazing and mysterious process.

The first few months without substances were very uncomfortable. I was stopped in my tracks during this transformation as I processed the reality of what had occurred. I felt naked and scared in my new world, invisible and without definition. My energy level was shifting, my thoughts were expanding and I could not put a lid on my growth. I wanted to deny that change had arrived. Yet, once my mind opened to the awareness that life was different, *it was*.

I began by changing one area of my life, and ended up creating more change and movement in surprising ways. As I slowed down and became aware of my feelings and thoughts, I realized that I wanted to move to a warmer climate with a slower pace of life.

Even though I was teaching in a community college and had what appeared to be a bright future, I realized that with the inner changes I was making, my outer life no longer fit. With this thought in mind, I left work, friends and my familiar community. I moved 500 miles south to an environment I thought would bring me peace.

I was determined to survive in early recovery with a minimum of temptations. To remain healthy I chose to be aware of my emotions, my thoughts, muscle movements, diet and how I handled conflict. I was glad I was moving forward, yet I cried for the old way of being, and became angry at my addiction and the loss that I now felt. Here I was, starting over once again.

When the awareness of change breaks through to reality, our needs and priorities — including our relationship to the universe — is thrown off course for a while. As we begin to sever those deeply held connections with our friends, family and community, we often start to mistrust our otherwise familiar world.

Many of us are called to change relationships, homes, careers and friendships in order to become self-actualizing. We can resist the signs of change, bury our head in the sand and try to control our emotions, or we can accept the reality of our lives.

Our first task in choosing awareness of change is to grieve and let go of our old way of being with people, places and things. Over the years we develop expectations from our daily habits, and many of us have to change our inner self by embracing our emotions rather than masking them with chemicals, food, relationships, sex, credit cards or gambling. When life no longer fits the patterns we've come to depend on, we grieve. We mourn our former communities and activities where we once felt we belonged. We grieve the loss of connection with friends, family and co-workers. Sometimes we must take a long hiatus from destructive relationships as we venture down our new path. We may grieve for the neighbor who always made us feel special or the child we watched grow year after year. As we move into a new realm, we become aware of our invisible connection to reality in our life.

Here we are confronted with this first choice of Fearless Change: *Let go* of the past and learn to trust the adventure. As we choose to accept what is true for us, we grow and experience the joys of life, no matter what has brought us to the healing path. We may feel excited and enthusiastic some days, or sad, with feelings of loss, despair and grief, on other days. Our interdependence on the balance of people, places, events and the energy of creation has been altered, impacting our emotions as well as our thoughts. (Refer to Fearless Change Map, page 6.) Regardless of the tone of the emotional roller coaster, we make the choice to be aware, reach outward to others and inward to our spirit. With help, we get through it.

Some of us tend to become distracted when our balance is off-kilter. We race from one thing to the next, not able to stay focused long enough to follow through with the process of change. We try to rush the process and become frustrated and overwhelmed when we can't move mountains at will. Others of us cope with the initial aspects of change by over-focusing on the things we can control. We might become obsessive, irritable and unable to see the larger view. We become critical of others and ourselves. To accept the challenge of change, we must learn to identify our own style of handling it. As we develop our faith and trust, we learn to meet and fulfill our needs in the best possible way and in the perfect time frame.

Sandra began developing trust after a six-month stay at a recovery center. She seemed to understand the big picture, but had difficulty dealing with the details. She wanted the perfect new home with the best roommates, a new boyfriend *and* she wanted to discover her purpose—all in the first month. These are reasonable and worthy goals, but achieving them within 30 days is about as likely as winning the lottery. When she returned to an alumni meeting at the recovery center, Sandra was told that she needed to work on taking life one day at a time. This was a challenge since she wasn't sure what to focus on first. Her sense of belonging and routine had been upset by her admission to the recovery center, the loss of her boyfriend, the healing that needed to take place with her family and the subsequent move to her apartment.

When Sandra left the center, she was indeed starting over again and her scattered feelings reflected her unmet need for grounding and consistency. She continued the journal writing she had begun in treatment and was able to understand through the dialog in her journal that her old boyfriend was unhealthy for her new life. Writing him a letter of good-bye, and for the first time truly meaning it, she thanked him for the opportunities the relationship provided for her to grow and learn more about herself. By seeing the challenges and pain as opportunities to learn, she blessed the experience and closed the door on that aspect of her past. Sandra realized that her primary relationship needed to be with her higher power first, her self, second and a relationship with a man, third.

Although she'd heard it before, her sponsor helped her see that she needed to start with the basics–getting comfortable in the new apartment with her new roommate. The first month she established routines that supported her recovery: She spent the first 15 minutes of the morning in her daily meditation, stretched, then created a schedule for the day to develop her routine and consistency. She located a 12-step meeting close to her home and stocked up on healthy foods. She liked to cook, so she invited some of the other women in her group to share in weekly potluck dinners. As she began to acquire a sense of inner strength, love and belonging, Sandra felt more committed to taking life-affirming actions such as walking each day and listening to the wisdom of those who were further down the recovery path. With more routines in place, and able to meet her needs within her own support system, Sandra was ready to begin the healing of her family relationships, and the discovery of her purpose. When she felt whole and complete, she would be drawn to a man who also felt healed. She had worked too hard on herself to begin dating before she was ready.

Awakening Trust

Those who are coming out of addiction or depression are often plagued by the thought, *"Why bother, what's the use?"* My biggest hurdle was to let go of my sense of futility and trust that I would find a compelling reason to hope.

When trust doesn't come easily, we have to develop it. Sandra felt fearful and unsure of herself when she first moved into her apartment until she reminded herself of the simple things she did have confidence in; that the sun will come up, that the laws of gravity are in place, that birds fly, dogs bark and she was safe. To strengthen our trust, we face our fearful thoughts and develop the voice of our inner faith. When chronic pain and addiction ran my life, I couldn't trust myself to keep my commitment to *not* use chemicals or *not* feel sorry for myself. Once I decided to trust my higher power to guide me through recovery, I discovered my hidden courage and strength. After the effects of the drugs wore off and I could see clearly, I realized that there was much in my life that I could not control or change.

Sandra, like me, struggled while she was learning the Serenity Prayer. She said it felt like a tongue twister. She couldn't seem to remember it because she didn't yet believe that she couldn't control the cravings of her body or the thoughts and actions of those she had relationships with. After several months, she found that her life ran smoothly when she was able to love unconditionally. She told me she finally let go of her catastrophic thinking and is now able to accept events as naturally occurring changes and opportunities.

The truth is that we can choose to feel love, faith and trust—or fear, pain and doubt—about the change we're going through. It just takes practice to feel safe and develop faith rather than bowing to our fears. Change is our opportunity to create a beautiful new chapter in our life of Fearless Change.

Letting Go

To let go of the past, starting five minutes ago, I detach from the fears, crazy thoughts and judgments. I am then free to be in the present moment where I can accept reality and take the necessary actions to move forward. It's important to heal our souls and acknowledge the loss of those people, routines or behaviors that gave us a sense of connection and belonging. Each loss needs its own form of resolution if we are to bless and say good-bye to the way things were.

I had a difficult time letting go of my mother's spirit after she died. I was unprepared for the impact her passing would have at that time in my life. She had stayed with me in spirit because I needed her, but when I realized that holding on was impeding my growth, I knew I had to let go.

Some friends who had a deeper understanding of death and the afterlife of the evolving spirit helped me to finally release her. I placed my mother's spirit in an empty chair as I prepared to say farewell. I told her how much I loved her, and how I had appreciated all she'd done for me. I recalled funny experiences, like when my brother put a peanut up his nose, and when the family cocker spaniel had a litter of puppies in the closet, and when we all shared a family picnic one rainy afternoon in the backseat of the family car, parked at a river's edge. I thanked her for the great orange-and-black skirt she made one Halloween, and for all the times she listened to the woes of a teenager in love. I also told her of the times I'd felt hurt when she hadn't protected me from my father's anger, and expressed my disappointed that we wouldn't be able to grow older together. I let her know that I would be moving in an uncertain direction, and that with the guidance of spirit, we would both be safe. I told her how much I'd miss her, and tearfully, with the prompting of my friends, told her I was releasing her spirit to move on to the next plane of her evolution. *Good-bye, Mom,* I said as I wept. *I love you. Good-bye Mommy.* And I felt her spirit leave me, softly and with love.

In the process of rebirth, letting go and releasing the spirit of someone we deeply love is not easy, yet it's an important part of moving on. I wouldn't want to go through the emotional pain of releasing my mother again, yet I know I wouldn't have been able to reach the same level of freedom and growth without that process. Who or what do you need to say good-bye to? Gather up your courage and make the choice to expand your personal power by releasing the past.

On occasion, the universe presents us with a healing opportunity that's masked as a crisis. At other times *we* decide when it's time to face our pain. We then walk through the memory to reclaim our strength.

My friend John was sad over the earlier losses in his life. His childhood dream of going to medical school was scratched when he lost the use of his arm in Vietnam. He said good-bye to his arm and his dreams, and eventually found joy in volunteering at a local military hospital.

Jean, a principal, let go of the joy and sadness she experienced after completing a project that put her school in the top academic bracket. Like many writers and actors who go through post-project let-down at the end of a creative endeavor, she felt the loss of being focused and involved, and discovered the need to set new goals for herself and her school.

As we weave together a new way of thinking, our emotions shift while we clear away whatever is blocking our spiritual path. We heal as we forgive others — and ourselves — for being human. And to forgive just once is often not enough. To realize all the benefits of forgiveness, we must continuously release the negative energy stored in our hearts and bodies, and transform it into light and love.

Healing the Past

The incomplete healing from our past distracts us from commitments in the present, and it's therefore helpful to find resolution. This split in our attention is the source of much agony. When we are in the present with our change and think about the past, we often project the emotional experience of that old event onto the present situation and imagine this current change will take the same path.

The reappearance of past wounds can help tweak our intuition. Recalling traumatic events can be the whisper we need to put our old unpleasant memories to rest, through acceptance and forgiveness. If more help is needed, seek out a licensed therapist to help you release the past. As we regain trust in ourselves, we grow in our spiritual journey. We learn to be more direct and assertive about what we need and don't need, and accept the limitations of being human. When we heal the emotions from the past, we allow the present to create it's own emotional experience with fresh thoughts to build on.

Our task is to understand how a particular situation has come to empower us. For example, you may have learned more about unconditional love from a failed romance and realized how your self-judgment was projected onto your partner and how you thought *he* or *she* said or did the *wrong* thing. You may have returned to college, done well and realized that your low grades in high school weren't due to a low I.Q., but rather to chaos at home or poor nutrition or drug use. Change stretches us to bring forth aspects of ourselves that were previously hidden and undeveloped.

Over the years I prayed and asked spirit for career direction, relationship resolution and guidance on how to reclaim my health. The answers came loud and clear: *"Love is the source of all life. Find unconditional love within yourself and others and know you are loved by spirit for exactly who you are. Express yourself."* I now had my mission—heal the past so I could live a full life. To dissolve illusions takes time and extreme conscious effort. As I listed all the things I was grateful for, I was more able to accept my current reality. Without gratitude, I create stress in my body as I resist reality. Then, if I'm not cautious about my intrusive thoughts and feelings, I end up with the heavy emotions of fear, guilt, remorse and resentment. If I don't release them, in time, I will become ill or depressed.

I began my journey more than 25 years ago and on occasion I've thought *if only such-and-such had happened, I wouldn't be going through this right now, my life would be different.* Then I'm stuck. With thoughts like that, I haven't yet gratefully acknowledged the good that fills my days. Like a clueless child,

I'm whining that there's not enough good stuff, when in truth I'm surrounded by it.

At this point on the Fearless Change Map, I stay on the left-hand side, and move up and down as I feel the loss and resist the change. I try to control myself and others, I feel stressed and confused as to why I feel so bad. When I mentally relive an experience, I blame myself or someone else rather than seeing that it's just "life." If I stay on the left side, I risk my progress in recovery. When I judge the loss of *what was* or what I think *could have been,* I fall into old survival habits that didn't help me then and definitely won't help me now. The illusions of our expectations create anger and resentment. When we think that we or someone else *should* or *could* act differently, we take ourselves out of reality. The problem is that we're focusing on something outside ourselves with the expectation that it will provide fantasies of how life ought to be.

If this is true for you, stop right now and think about the flow of your change.

1. What aspect of my life do I need to accept for today?

2. What or who could I release today?

3. Do I forgive others and myself for this change?

4. How am I saying good-bye?

Embrace the Adventure

To honor our commitment to grow we can accept reality without judging or wishing it were different, or we can stay in our pain. Even if we initiate change, we must get beyond the loss of what was known and accept today's reality. Many people stay in unpleasant situations because they'd rather face *"the demons we know."* The unknown is always disconcerting at best, downright scary at worst. We don't need to like what's happened, or the reasons why we're now on the brink. What we do need to know is that the past is written in cement. Sorry, no revisions. This decision takes courage as we allow ourselves to practice this first choice of Fearless Change: *Let go* of what is no longer.

Most of us imagine we enjoyed the comfort of what was, even with all its frustrations and difficulties. Once the honeymoon is over in a relationship, we grieve for the lost thrill of infatuation and bonding. We say good-bye to the alcohol that used to be our friend, to the career that no longer works, to our once-youthful body, to the child who's become an adult, to the aging parent who has lost her memory. We think we'd love our partner or our children more *if only* we could return to those better times. We would love them more if they'd take more or less responsibility, be more romantic, lose weight, give us more attention or humor us *just because.* Once we can accept that there are phases and developmental challenges in all relationships, moving through inevitable change is less painful.

This awareness of our change marks the death of what was and announces the birth of new ideas. Alexander Graham Bell, the ingenious inventor of the telephone, once said, *"When one door closes another door opens; but we so often look so long and so regretfully upon the closed door, that we do not see the ones which open for us."* Our emotional self gets scared in the hallway. It's here that we shed the skins of our old selves and leave them behind. We have not renounced our true selves, only that part which is not for our highest good right now. To move forward we claim our confidence, our voice and our truth through our commitment to walk through the next open door.

The Fearless Change process reinvents our perceptions of life and is designed as a guide for those long, dark tunnels of transition. Practice the choices and discover ways to trust the positive side of the process. Grow in your confidence and receive the respect from others that you didn't get at home. Begin to understand the true meaning of prosperity. Learn that being alone isn't synonymous with loneliness or abandonment. Understand that change is movement in our souls, active in the process of creation.

If we have learned and used this choice, to let go of our attachment to that which is no longer, we move on to the next choice. We feel the renewed sense of trust and acceptance. We have recognized our change, grieved for our losses and made a conscious choice to let go of those things that no longer support us. Bless what has been, even if it's brought you pain. Release your hurts and reclaim your energy as you move to the next choice of Fearless Change. Know you are adequate and begin to trust in the power of the universe to meet your needs.

The great thing about accepting our adventure is the wonder we arouse in ourselves. Through change we become more confident in our self-esteem and our ability to form and maintain relationships, and are open to different ways of doing everything. When we've been able to let go fully, to accept change as an important aspect of our spiritual journey, and forgive ourselves as well as others, we then begin to see it as the divine intervention it is. Free to move forward, we celebrate the transition and honor the passing of the old and the arrival of the new.

As St. Augustine said, *"God provides the wind, but man must raise the sails."* We are on to the next leg of our voyage. ➤

Chapter 8

Choose to Explore Options

"The difficulty in life is the choice."

— George Moore, Irish writer

The second Choice of Fearless Change is to *Explore and Define our Options.* This choice offers us opportunities to learn courage and willingness. Exploring is my favorite phase of the Fearless Change process! I love to learn new things and investigate all possibilities. By choosing to explore the unknown, I discover options and increase my trust that a new door will open, somewhere. I am certain that my newly discovered needs will be fulfilled.

I began my spiritual journey because I felt empty. I was unaware that my physical pain was a symptom of my emotional ache and spiritual deprivation. I felt alone and thought I was being punished, although I wasn't quite certain for what. I knew my neighbor was a Christian Scientist and that she prayed in a way to not feel pain, so I asked her to help me to understand how she did it. She willingly shared her knowledge and books with me about how to heal from the inside out. I learned to connect to spirit, realize that I was never empty, and change my thoughts and images through reading, praying, visualizing and affirming the omnipresent power of the universe. I also developed a better understanding of God, the force of life that brings me comfort today. This exploration awakened my curiosity and led me to study many different religions and spiritual traditions.

Through having learned the first choice of Fearless Change, *acceptance of what is no longer,* be it a belief, person, lifestyle, job or home, we free up energy to reinvent our life. As we step into the unknown we investigate and connect with new ideas, experiences and groups of people. The choice to explore awakens our inner being and gives us an understanding of our purpose, which adds meaning and richness to our day-to-day experiences. We look for signs that validate our journey. We find coincidences that appear out of the blue, assurances that we are on track. We might meet with an old friend, recall an old pal and receive a letter from him, or gaze at a new spring blossom. All have special meaning if we allow ourselves to explore the depth of our soul.

With this choice, we find healthy avenues to fulfill our basic human needs. In the process we increase our self-esteem; improve relationships, balance our work, creative expression and acquire a sense of belonging. We make discoveries about the *new* by reading books, traveling, attending workshops or lectures and establishing new friendships. We find healthy, positive ways to feel good about ourselves, and a strong network of groups and individuals who will empower us to grow.

If we resist this facet of the change, we tend to deny our needs, avoid setting goals or expanding our lives to fill the void created by change. We don't realize that we need something until we find ourselves in the middle of the left-hand side of the Fearless Change Map. We feel overwhelmed and angry as we try to manage what's impossible to control; then feel the resentment caused by our unmet expectations.

We may be irritable and frustrated because of a physical, mental or emotional injury or illness. We realize the need to reinvent our health or our career, yet we don't know where to turn. The solution often comes when we call others for support, pray or focus on the solution rather than the problem, and release either ourselves or someone else with acceptance and forgiveness. Finding a solution takes cooperation with the universe of people, places, things, time and the energy of creation.

In his senior year of high school, Michael was injured in a sporting activity. The incident resulted in abdominal injuries and he was under a doctor's care for over two years. He became so fascinated with the inner workings of his body that he ended up in medical school. Releasing the resentment freed his mind to find alternate ways to understand suffering. Michael's injuries ultimately taught him to become a skilled and caring physician.

Healing the Emotion of Anger

When we feel anger over unmet needs, it's helpful to discover healthy ways to reframe and express our feelings. If we repress our emotions we distort our power and it emerges as self-denial, illness, exhaustion, depression or aggression. On the other hand, to laugh, sing, write, play an instrument, listen to music, exercise, ride a bike, dance or paint transforms the intense energy of anger into laughter and joy. Physical and emotional exercise changes our internal chemistry and keeps our stress level down. Creative expression frees our soul to go about its purpose: to learn and to love.

As you explore and define your options, it helps to list positive and energizing experiences from your past. To reinvent my life I wanted to find people who were interested in similar activities. I'd learned that similar interests and values formed a foundation for friendship, love and career satisfaction. With close friendships we can expose our vulnerable self and gain inner strength from the exchange.

Memory and Emotions

Some of us may resist the need to reach out to others because we don't feel the world is safe. As we begin to change and fulfill our quest for self-esteem and creative potential, we wonder if the new *really* will show up, or if we'll be alone with these challenges forever. We may see life in terms of absolutes; all-or-nothing thinking, until we're able to trust the process of creation.

Many of us have experienced an earlier ordeal, and the memories may resurface at this time. That can inhibit our ability to seek guidance from our usual support system. Jerry became anxious and was experiencing panic attacks and his co-worker gave him my number. Through our talking, Jerry disclosed that he was resistant to tell his wife how sad he was when he heard there was going to be a lay-off at work. When he was growing up, to show sadness was considered weakness and Jerry would have been beaten by his dad. The injuries we incur unconsciously bind us to traumatic memories, and we don't realize all the emotions that are unavailable to us. These wounds have created scars that block awareness of our needs, so we must find alternative ways to heal the fear and shame that have hindered our growth and our ability to find love and joy.

If we've resisted the exploration of our deeper selves, we may have focused instead on trying to control what others say or do. If this is the case, now is the time to practice the second choice of Fearless Change: *Explore other options*. Learn to reframe the thoughts and behaviors you have developed on the Path of Fear, set goals to help you avoid the misconception that you have control over others and focus on being more cooperative. If we feel responsible *for* others, rather than *to* others, it's because of an imagined sense of duty. As parents, partners, children, siblings, friends, employers and employees, we have an investment in how well others do, and we often become frustrated if *they* don't meet our expectations. We may cover for them in different ways to avoid their defensiveness when we ask that they be responsible. To make others dependent on us is unhealthy—for everyone.

As we continue to practice the first choice, we detach and *let go* and remember that experience teaches responsibility. We give advice when asked, rather than believing we're responsible for all the answers, and we understand that it's healthy to be responsible *to* rather than *for* others. We practice *interdependence* rather than dependence or independence, the extremes of the continuum.

Dependent   ⟷   Interdependent   ⟷   Independent

When I'm responsible to my family, I allow them to make choices, and I accept that even though they may not do something my way, their way is okay. As I accept that they do things differently, I reinforce my new belief that life is filled with shades of gray. The difference is that we're responsible for helping others when they're in physical danger, especially the young and elderly, or to others when they ask. Otherwise our micro-management results in attempts to manipulate others because we fear that our needs for personal power won't be met any other way.

Paula enrolled in a Fearless Change workshop because she'd been depressed and drifting. She lacked the enthusiasm to reach out and create a more rewarding life. She'd been raised in an abusive family that considered God to be punishing and judgmental, where love was conditional, mistakes were tantamount to failure and emotional pain was denied. When she finally identified her unmet needs, she came to realize that she was fearful of love and had difficulty with trust in an intimate relationship. Paula came to understand that the anxiety she felt when she was around her friend, Christopher, was also the excitement of love. By telling Christopher how she felt, she was able to remind herself that she was safe. And he no longer had to interpret her reticence as unexpressed anger and rejection. Her power to protect herself, taken from her as a child, was reawakened. As Paula reclaimed her power, she developed a healthy spiritual connection. She was willing to explore her options, find her courage and take a risk to move beyond past hurts.

As we accept the reality of all aspects of our lives, we're better able to define priorities. To take action and do what we must to support our changed priorities may provoke intense emotions. But when we exercise our power of choice, we're reminded that we are valuable and do have a sense of control over our lives. We reinvent ourselves in the present moment by being conscious of the oxygen we breathe and the quality of our thoughts. We are the only ones who have the control to create positive, beautiful images and take positive actions. These shifts create an emotional state in which we experience peace, serenity and joy. We gain knowledge as we seek to understand the higher order of spiritual connection, rather than be guided by the old worn-out beliefs of our past.

If you find yourself challenged by the change in your life, take the leap to the Reframe box and reinvent your life. Reframe your situation into something you can accept—or better yet, something you can embrace with joy.

Actions for Growth

Try this:
1. Ask yourself what you need right now and what you can do within the next thirty minutes. It might be something as simple as getting a drink of water, eating a snack, calling someone, taking a jacket to the cleaners, making an overdue dental appointment, or signing up for a class. Now, *do it!* (Then pat yourself on the back or treat yourself to a small but meaningful reward.)

2. Identify your shadow. If you're judging someone else, ask yourself which of his or her qualities remind you of yourself.

3. Develop your empathy. Ask yourself how you might better understand a particular person and what he or she is going through right now.

4. Share your response to someone's behavior or comments. If there's a problem, let the other person know what would work better for you. For example: *When you speak softer and slower, I'm more apt to hear and understand you.*

5. Be aware of how your feelings may be compounded by past or current issues. Think back to the earliest time you felt a particular emotion and write or talk about it.

6. Unresolved power struggles from childhood, usually stemming from a lack of positive attention, often get played out in our adult relationships or with our children.

Choose to disengage, listen carefully and respond with a hug instead.

7. Feeling overwhelmed? Choose to stop. Count to ten and ask spirit to show you a different way to respond to the challenge. Look for solutions rather than letting yourself be overwhelmed by problems.

8. Think about life in shades of gray rather than black and white. Instead of judging a person or situation, say to yourself, "That's an interesting way to look at it."

9. Today, if you complain that you're not getting enough of something, ask yourself if you're *giving* it.

10. Compose a gratitude list today and remind yourself of what's *right* in your day rather than what's wrong or missing.

To utilize our personal power we choose to reframe our thoughts to give us a new perspective on the situation. We create trust and love in our relationships without compromising ourselves in exchange for attention or approval. We begin to see life as safe and in divine order. We're able to use our voice, show kindness, describe our dreams and say "yes" to our heart.

Calmness returns when we accept what's taken place, assume responsibility for adjusting to it and make the most of our experience. As writer Patricia Dark says, *"Knowing the tide will turn following each storm is wisdom. Seeking hope in the midst of pain is faith. Awaiting good to flow is patience."* When we are in agreement with ourselves, we seek and find harmony in the world. ➤

Chapter 9

Choose to Talk to Others

*"Nothing you undertake with certain purpose and high resolve
and happy confidence, holding to your brother's hand and
keeping step to Heaven's song, is difficult to do."*

— *A Course in Miracles*

When I need to make this choice of change, I realize it's because I'm isolating myself and my thoughts are confusing. Like driving down the freeway with one foot on the gas and one on the brake, I'm not going anywhere, just moving in place and burning up energy. I'm stressed and frustrated and I bounce between extremes. One day I'm so motivated and enthusiastic I can't sleep at night. The next day I'm sure I'm doomed to failure and want to pull the covers over my head and stay in bed. If I do get up, I shed tears of frustration when I can't open a jar or find a place to park. My perfectionism dominates and I overanalyze every possible pitfall. I doubt my intuition and stress over what to do. I run through a multitude of scenarios. *If I do this, then that (either wonderful or horrible) will happen.* My perceived outcome may waffle between grandiose and disastrous, and I don't know what will happen unless I take action. I have to remind myself that my higher power is in charge, anyway. The only control I actually have is what I think about as I step into the void of the day. Talking with others helps me to process my thoughts and receive ideas that connect me to the greater whole.

As we move along in the change process, we create a blueprint for our growth. In the first two choices, we learned to *let go* of those things that we are not in charge of, and we *explored our options* by examining other pathways. In the third choice we develop a positive belief and support system as we learn to reframe our thinking. With motivation we take daily action toward our vision of the new, while surrendering the outcome to the power of the universe.

My friend Tracy was feeling lonely and disconnected one night and decided to call a reputable prayer line. She asked in prayer for supportive people to give her some help. Soon after the prayer session she received a phone call from a woman she'd met briefly the month before and was invited to join a volunteer organization to make blankets for needy children. From there she met others who helped her and soon her loneliness evaporated as her activities soared.

Our thoughts impact the way we respond to the people, places and things we encounter. Since the energy of creation responds to what we think and truly need by reflecting life back to us, we want to stabilize our thoughts and feelings in a positive way. Expect the best! We can create wonderful visions about what we're *going* to do someday, or what we *would like* to do, *if only____*. But until we take action we have little chance of bringing what we need into our reality.

Sometimes we're uncertain where to go, and what to do. To isolate our energy during this part of a change is normal. We don't want to make a mistake. But sometimes we're so afraid of failing that we isolate and do nothing at all. In short, we're trying too hard to control the situation.

Gather Positive Support

Years ago when I felt my recovery was stable enough, I had a better understanding of what I needed and wanted in relationships. I was determined to use my assertiveness skills and set boundaries so I would not compromise myself. To honor my values and integrity, I listened to my inner self with respect, which was something I hadn't done for a while. I thought about past relationships and made a list of the qualities I enjoyed and admired, and those traits that didn't work for me. I recalled the feelings I'd had in positive friendships. Patty, my friend since the eighth grade, truly listens to me and thinks I get along well with people. Even to this day, she's someone I trust. Michele brought out my sense of fun and adventure. Darcy gave me positive feedback on my creative ideas and the way I looked at the world.

I wrote out a list of the qualities that helped me to feel good about myself and created the affirmation, *I am attracting new, trustworthy friends. They listen, share adventures and value the way I look at the world.* One by one, I rekindled old friendships and developed new ones with women who are supportive and positive. The time we spend together is inspiring.

Then I decided to write the same type of list to help me develop a relationship with a man. I listed twenty-five qualities I felt were important in an intimate relationship. Each morning and evening I read the list and affirmed that the universe would draw me closer to him, as I surrendered the outcome to divine providence. I trusted that some day this mystery man would show up or not, depending on what was best for all concerned.

In the meantime I went about my life, had fun with my friends, continued to work on my issues and developed my interests. I did my inner spiritual work, read, prayed and meditated. My friends gave me the external positive support I needed. I learned to enjoy creative meal planning, movies, plays, weekend trips and quiet afternoons painting, sewing, cooking and learning something new.

The wonderful people I've met at support group meetings and work events, my current and former neighbors, co-workers, employees and employers, today enrich my life. Each person gives me a sense of connection as he or she reflects a different aspect of who I am. When I reach out to my friends Lesah, Judy, Kathryn, Sana, Kay or Wilna I receive the strength of their insights. My support system sees me differently than I see myself, and for this I'm grateful! To isolate creates tunnel vision and I forget the multifaceted aspects of my life.

I was just now on the phone with the wife of a former client. Her husband had relapsed a few months ago and although she knew that she could help herself by going to a support group meeting, she wanted my validation that this was the best thing to do. She had been staying away from friends, ignoring her husband's lies and her own sadness. As she hung up, she knew that I would keep them both in my thoughts. She unknowingly practiced this third choice of Fearless Change: She reached out to others to help her reframe her thinking toward a more positive vision.

We help ourselves and others to grow as we allow ourselves to move with the energy of life. The universe is a field of dynamic energy and continuous change, and we must get in step and move with it. Answers to our innermost questions and challenges are revealed through this magical dance.

Larry came for counseling because he was struggling with his lack of enthusiasm at work. He couldn't sustain his motivation and felt isolated from others because he was afraid of their judgments. He'd been diagnosed as depressed or attention-deficit disordered for much of his seven years of recovery. Together we determined that part of his problem was an issue he'd left unresolved during the change process. He had been in a business partnership that had gone bankrupt prior to his recovery and had wiped out his financial investment. He was hesitant to start a business again, yet he needed to do something that was both fulfilling and financially viable. Since he didn't like working for others, Larry wanted to give himself permission to reclaim his dream and try again.

I could see where he was stuck on the Choices of Change Chart and I asked him to go back to the first choice — letting go of what was no longer. Larry decided to stop blaming his partner for the business failure. He wrote him a letter and outlined the challenges of their partnership, owned up to his part in the experience and apologized. As he mailed the letter he discovered that this was an opportunity to learn a priceless lesson about taking responsibility. This faith gave him the energy to accept the adventure of change.

Next, he looked at the second choice and identified which of his needs were unmet. Besides seeking to fulfill himself vocationally, Larry wanted to balance his physical needs by eating healthier and exercising regularly rather than sporadically. He discovered that the structure of a morning walk gave him time to think about what he wanted to accomplish for the day. Larry's self-respect was slumping because he'd been judging himself harshly. While he was exploring his options, he read stories of others who had succeeded in business after some rough beginnings. By starting another venture, Larry felt he would be able to respect himself and fulfill an important emotional need. He recalled his childhood dream to make specialized auto parts for race cars. As a child he would go to the track with his uncle and watch the cars for hours. Thinking about auto racing again brought out the kid in him. This also triggered issues of feeling passive as a child and unable to ask for what he wanted. Applying the choices of Fearless Change, he could now face the unknown with assertiveness.

As he practiced asking for what he wanted, Larry came to understand that assertive communication is the link to our interdependence on people, situations and events. He then made contact with someone in a similar business who could be a mentor and coach. Larry called him once a week and reported on his progress while he explored his options. He worked on developing positive beliefs as he read daily inspirational meditations. He said affirmations aloud each day, listened to motivational tapes, and joined a support group to help him stick to an eating plan. Rather than just thinking about what he was going to do and feeling restricted by a lack of information, Larry took positive action and got results.

After we identify our needs we're ready to proceed. Many of us get out of balance during this difficult emotional period. Old doors have closed and we're in the hallway and only vaguely see the image of the new passageway. Still cautious about the unknown, we'd like to believe that something good is waiting for us. We set our goals, write down what we would like to experience in our new relationship, career or lifestyle, think positively throughout the day, and take action while we surrender the results to spirit. Our mission is to welcome and embrace whatever waits for us behind the next door.

Show up Believing

Once we truly realize that we're not in control of the life force (the basis of the change), we can go ahead and surrender the challenge to our higher power. Or we can feel helpless and think, *"What's the use – why bother?"* There is always a choice.

If we're assertive in our inner communication, we ask the universe that our needs be met, step into action and stop trying to control the outcome. Even if we don't know whether it's the *right* choice, we still need to take steps to begin the process. The signs along the way will guide us. That's where trust comes in. For some of us, optimism is something we have to practice each day. Many of us have experienced depression and trauma either in our family life, through injuries, accidents, military experiences, work or illness. As a result, our point of view may be tainted by feelings of futility or outright despair. It takes time to reframe our perception to *this is going to be a great day...I look forward to the unknown...it's all going to work out.*

I was told that I was a negative thinker from the time I was eight years old. Reframing my thoughts to be positive took time and effort, and I still have slips now and then. Consider the metaphor of positive thinking as a new language: If we don't practice regularly, we lose our fluency. When I'm optimistic I move forward with ease, taking challenges in stride and seeing them as opportunities.

Our positive images will guide us in the right direction, whether it's toward increased assertiveness, healing from a loss, finding a more fulfilling career, inventing a better mousetrap or creating a new vision of our health.

When we are in the flow of life and trust the abundant wellspring of new ideas, projects, jobs, friendships and opportunities just waiting for us, we feel energized and motivated. We easily tap our energy and open to the creative flow in our lives. As the energy emerges, we feel it for a few minutes, then a few hours, a few days and then for longer periods of time. But we may feel discouraged when it doesn't appear to be long lasting. But wait! If we have isolated for a long time, the flow of motivational energy will take time to work in and through our well-entrenched stumbling blocks.

Actions for Growth

Try this:

1. Keep an affirmation or prayer next to your alarm clock and as you roll over to turn off the buzzer, jump-start your positive motivation for the day by reading it over three or four times. Start the day on the right side of the bed—on a positive track.

2. Do daily soul strengthening exercises for ten minutes each morning, with large doses of inspirational reading and tapes.

3. Read the inspiration aloud, slowly and with feeling, as if the words were the truest ones you've ever heard.

4. Keep a list of your goals. Take five minutes when you sit down at your computer or with your journal, and write out your affirmations and the progress you've made toward your goals.

5. Speak your affirmation aloud, with emotion; then write it, draw it, visualize it—and then let go of the outcome.

6. Letting go: Place your written goal or good-bye message in a holy book, or tuck it away in a special spot. Like a seedling, it is now germinating.

7.   Act as if your good is on its way, and go about your other activities to keep yourself in balance.

8.   Cut out images that represent your desired outcome and tape them up along with your affirmations, on your bathroom mirror, refrigerator, dashboard, or inside your purse, wallet, checkbook or organizer. Surround yourself with reminders to think positively.

9.   As you affirm aloud that you're experiencing your goal right now, you create the feelings that draw it, or something even better, toward you. To integrate the changes in our beliefs and stay positive when we're anxious, we need to get to the deepest levels of our being. When you repeatedly practice reframing your struggles as challenges, opportunities and blessings in disguise, you'll stay in touch with your enthusiasm.

When I get to this choice in my own life, I do my affirmations and double up on inspirational reading. And–I do things I enjoy. I talk to others who inspire me, I write e-mail or letters, call old friends, make lunch dates and join in uplifting group activities. I am sensitive to the energy of others and cautious about exposing myself to negativity. Stay in the light of the positive, even if you have to leave a group or certain people for a while. You can't afford to have your energy drained.

We begin change today by taking action now. Contact someone or something that will propel you into the creative flow. As my cousin, Stewart, a screenwriter and movie producer, always reminds me, "*It's already done in the future. You just have to catch up to it.*" Or, as one 12 step member I know says, "*Eighty-five percent of life is just showing up.*" So all we need to do is *show up,* believing everything we need is in place. Here are some examples of reframed thoughts:

Old Thought	**Reframe As:**
I shouldn't, because I don't have enough money.	*I choose to use my money for other priorities.*
I can't because I don't know how.	*I choose the excitement of learning something new.*
I don't have enough time.	*I choose to spend my time on higher priorities.*
I can't change because this is all I've ever done.	*I choose to take the risk to do things differently.*
I have to____ because of my ____.	*I choose my own top priority right now.*
I can't _____because I'm too old.	*I choose to believe that I'm as young as I feel.*

To believe that everything manifests in divine order—and even better than we imagined—is the foundation of Fearless Change. If you're like many other people I know, you may have tried affirmations and haven't seen the results you'd hoped for. If other approaches haven't produced acceptable results, why not try this?

There are plenty of things we do trust and have faith in. Sometimes only one particular issue may have us stumped. To move into trust on the issue at hand requires that we reframe our thinking, access our inner imagery and change our feelings. The negative old thoughts, *I shouldn't because I don't have enough money or time; this is all I've ever done; I don't know how*; or *I'm too old*, keep us from feeling good about ourselves and moving forward.

Statements like *I can't, I shouldn't* and *I have to* surface when our unconscious believes we are lacking, or when we fear either failure or success.

Choose Renewal

In declaring that we have choice, we actually announce that we *will* do or *are* doing something differently. In the middle of our traumatic memories or addiction, we're without choice and we make decisions in the moment with our trauma or addiction having the highest priority. In the process of reclaiming our health, our priorities are reordered. We now have the opportunity to review our options and make healthy choices. Refer back to the Characteristics of Relationships Chart on page 22. You can see that as we reframe our old beliefs, we shift our perception of our world.

As I step into action I have emotional responses to that which seems unfamiliar. If I react with old behaviors, I'll look through the list of beliefs to see if I have an old fear-based thought that needs to be reframed into trust. To listen to and honor our emotions is a powerful step toward positive growth. Discover your strength and courage as you counter the scars of trauma with memories of pleasure, optimism and self-respect.

When we discover pleasure, our internal motivation, we add joy and richness to our days. Our pleasurable experiences from earlier times feel as rich as if they happened yesterday. We all have these peak experiences growing up; they're the ones that help us survive during the bad times.

When Richard was a boy, he rode his bike for miles after school so he wouldn't have to go home to his crazy mother. His healthy escape motivated him so much that years later he organized a bike-riding club. Besides all the physical benefits, the club provides a wonderful and positive support system for Richard and his companions.

Yolanda loved putting on plays and musicals with neighborhood kids; it was her way of avoiding the chaos of alcoholism in her family. She still uses these skills today in her preschool classes.

Be Willing

With this part of the change, I ask myself what I'm risking: my fear of rejection, of being overwhelmed, of failure, of shame and humiliation, of financial ruin? Life is risky. Be willing to stretch and take the leap of faith to reframe and reinvent your life.

As I learn to reframe my fears, my life takes on new meaning and purpose. I feel protected as I surround myself with an invisible bubble, created from the indestructible strength of my higher power. I'm then safe to pursue my goals and positive expectations. I meditate and read inspirational words to help keep my spiritual core calm and centered, like the eye of the storm. Daily, I practice saying, *"With God's help, anything is possible. I am willing to do whatever it takes to grow through this change."* I put affirmations, prayers, reasons for the change, and statements of willingness in my pocket, on my walls and in my car to help my ever-wandering mind stay on track. I remind myself that I'm going to get through it all and that this change will result in something positive—and maybe even wonderful.

Another way to sustain my motivation is to reframe thoughts of emotional neediness.

Old Thought	Reframe As:
I don't know what to do.	*There is always an answer and I'll quiet my mind so I can hear it.*
Why bother – what's the use?	*I am valuable, strong, and I belong. Today is a new beginning.*
I've been such a fool, nothing good will ever happen to me again.	*Something good will come out of this. Good things are happening to me right now.*
I blew it.	*A mistake is a great opportunity to learn. I am on my perfect path, learning exactly what I need.*

Internal Motivation Empowers Our Healing

I find that by creating a blueprint for change I channel the energy released from forgiving, through *letting go*. Having learned to explore my options, I reframe my loss and discover my willingness to cooperate with the universe; I talk to others and hear in return the guidance I need. I become willing to do whatever it takes to go forward.

Being a feeling-oriented person, I like to find healthy expression for this emotional energy. Emotional energy is non-verbal and responds to music, dance, writing, art, painting, sculpting, drawing, singing, yoga, exercise and laughter. Emotional expression is crucial for integrating change. If it's not expressed through action, the energy will be repressed and can reappear in a negative way. This is no longer an option for me. I choose to keep discovering and expressing my emotional energy.

At this point in their change, people often enter therapy because they don't know what they really feel or need. The goals of therapy are often to find expression and resolution for deeply buried losses. Accepting and forgiving our distant past allows us to let go of our recent past and gives us access to our emotions in the here and now so we can move on with positive expectations.

With a positive belief and support system, we see our cup as half full—and getting fuller each day! As we reaffirm our commitment to grow and heal, we strengthen or build a new support system. We return to healthy eating and responsible financial management. We meditate and seek guidance from the center of our being, where balance and inner strength coexist. We are hopeful, grateful and find ourselves thinking, *"I'm glad I learned about___. This is working out great!"* Our emotions are more responsive, we ask questions, and are open to new people, situations, information and ideas that emerge from the energy of the universe. One anonymous philosopher posed the question of motivation this way: *"Am I willing to give up what I have in order to be what I am not yet? Am I willing to let go of my ideas of myself, of others, and be changed?"* ➤

Chapter 10

Choose to Grow
Healthy Habits

"Press toward the mark of the prize of the higher calling. "

—Philippians 3:14

I began to use visualization—the conscious use of imagination—to change my habitual thoughts and behaviors many years ago to ease the chronic pain in my back in legs. The doctors had told me there was no way to ease the pain, that the situation was inoperable and would only get worse with age. They said to just take pain pills *as needed,* and accept the fact that I couldn't work, walk or have the life I wanted. In those days my imagery reflected my feelings of sorrow, powerlessness and victimization. Just in my early thirties, I saw myself living the life of an eighty-year-old woman.

As I changed my self-concept from martyrdom to the vision of what I *really* wanted to be, I began reaching out to people, books and tapes to learn the techniques of visualization. I meditated and quieted the old helpless images that held my mind hostage. This allowed me to visualize pictures of strength, confidence and healing light surrounding the cells in my spine. Whenever I showered, I envisioned myself walking briskly, my body swaying to the seductive rhythm of a jazz tune. And I saw myself — having fun! While I was fixing breakfast I visualized my muscles working together like an integrated team. As I shifted my mental and physical habits, life began to change, and I had a new and empowering paradigm to express my values, ideas and vision.

As I draw from these images that are now an integral part of me, I find myself automatically thinking holistically about my body. The language of mental pictures is often more powerful than words.

Imagination, Habits and Growth

All ideas are good because they spark our creative flow. Continuing to be creative generates growth and pleasure. Imagination is connected to our nonverbal self, the emotional, intuitive and spiritual being that resides deep within. As we develop our imagination, we create new solutions to overcome feelings of helplessness or martyrdom. I've continued to use my imagination to help me find jobs, meet new people, overcome test anxiety and panic attacks, quit smoking, start a business, write a book, draw a wonderful man into my life and become a parent.

Our imagination, that magnificent, divine creative energy, is ready to burst forth with new ideas, emotions and experiences as we move into this phase of change. Our senses resemble the first scent of spring, awakened after the stillness of winter. We smell, see, hear and taste the new beginning. After we have let go of the old, explored our options and tapped our motivation, we now add habits that support those new aspects. These new thought patterns soon comprise our current reality. So in order to grow, we must become aware of our blueprint for thinking, our voice tone and intention.

Habits are rituals that give us a sense of control over our lives. They are the managers of our dynamic life force, and they either empower us, keeping us healthy and safe, or act as a saboteur. Habits are essential to our daily functioning, setting us on autopilot, so we can carry out the details of our life without conscious effort. For example, when we brush our teeth, we don't consciously think: Now I'm picking up my toothbrush, now I'm applying the toothpaste, now I'm massaging my teeth and gums. If we had to concentrate on the hundreds of tiny, automatic actions that make up our daily lives, we'd never get anything done. Yet we have a responsibility to ourselves to become more aware of what we do, and the choices we make. When you spend moments today being conscious of each action you undertake, you'll notice how much your awareness increases of other choices in your life as well.

We can choose to become aware of our important thoughts and actions, and gain a sense of control over our health, moods, and interactions. When I learned to accept the people and things in my environment, I changed my habit of reacting explosively, either internally or externally, when I was fearful, sad or guilty. And I changed my habit of expecting that I, or others, *should* be saying or doing something differently.

In the earlier aspects of dramatic change, our habits are uprooted and we have a chance to take control and become aware of what we do with our new choices and patterns. Some habits, such as exercising, eating well and practicing good hygiene, support our physical and emotional well-being. Other habits, such as smoking, inactivity and gorging on junk food are destructive. Each action we take, no matter how minute, brings forth a consequence. For example, sitting down next to an ashtray may trigger the old thought process, *look for cigarettes and matches*. And if we're not careful, we continue down that pathway, find the cigarette (just one!) and puff away.

Research has found that people are more successful at adding new habits than eliminating old ones. And practicing a new behavior or thought process each day for just 21 days gives you the power to transform your relationships as well as your mental and physical health. So replace that treacherous ashtray with a bowl of fruit and set your walking shoes in front of the recliner. Have an apple and go for a walk before you sit down and smoke your cigarette. You are offering the addicted self a chance to build a different habit. Now is the time to become aware of your negative patterns and replace them with beneficial routines. Physical action creates the chemical changes in our brain that supports creativity. As you probably know, exercise is a well-known method of combating mild depression and lethargy. When we maintain nutritional wellness through balanced eating, we give ourselves the energy necessary to sustain our motivation—a vital aspect of change.

Awareness of our habits puts us in touch with our decision to live a full life. It helps us tune in to our internal and external words, which underlie the emotional tone of our communications. We realize what we need, and we ask for it before we fall back into the old martyr-like syndrome of *poor me*. This awareness encourages us to be responsible for who we are and what we create.

During times of change, I've found myself easily distracted, establishing habits that don't work for me. I went through multiple transformations when my daughter was born, when my husband changed careers and when I moved my office closer to home. I was determined to reinvent my practice, keep different hours, and meet people in my new location. I wanted to write and give workshops, but I felt stuck. The problem was that each morning I pulled numerous projects out of the drawer and tried to tackle them all at once. I was overwhelmed. I was talking to God much of the time, but my mind was so cluttered that I couldn't really listen to my possible options. Once in a while a light bulb would go off and ideas would start to flow, yet I couldn't seem to stay with the visualization I'd created. I wanted to see myself working and completing one project at a time, but I lacked the focus and follow-through.

Lesah, a friend who is a corporate trainer, sent me a birthday gift. She was unaware that inside the box, on a piece of paper she'd used in one of her courses, was another, even more precious gift. The paper read, "Organize, Prioritize and Follow Through." The message was loud and clear: I had to change my organizational habits before I could make any effective changes. God sometimes gets our attention in funny ways. Even though I'd been letting go of the past with my thoughts and emotions, I hadn't yet adjusted my external environment. So I reorganized my space, cleared out drawers in the office, house and in the garage, and gave away as much clutter as I could in order to simplify my life. I created a space where the old used to be, so my new creative energy would have room for expression.

We are empowered when we can do those things that keep us strong and healthy in our bodies, emotions and spirit. I make a list of the things I like to do for fun—and then I do them. I spend time with people who think positively and are supportive of my change. I used to have ideas that I would discount with thoughts such as *I can't do that* or *that seems kind of silly.* I now carry a notebook with me, and sometimes while driving, I pull over just to jot down an idea.

I enjoy the habit of reading inspirational meditations in the early morning. It keeps me grounded in the present while I allow my creative self to surge forward with the new day. I keep a box of crayons and colored pens next to me to allow spirit to work through me to express ideas, feelings and lists of possibilities.

With these activities, we gain insight and clarity, which strengthens our sense of personal power. I have found that the more detailed my vision, the more efficiently the universe is in manifesting the results. Flashes of creativity will often emerge after a dream, in the shower or while doing something that gives us pleasure. Write down *all* your ideas, even if you think you'll remember them, have written them out before or even if you're not sure they're worthwhile. Using my imagination, I think about how I can create a life rich in friends, contribution, laughter, adventure and love. I visualize my future and have created a goal book. I collect various images and photos of a healthy body, friends and family, exotic travel and lists of topics I want to explore. I visualize myself energized, in the creative stream, meeting life with joy. I stimulate the new by saying aloud the words of my new choices; I sing them or shout them to the wind. To awaken even deeper levels of my emotions, I listen to unusual music, smell a variety of aromas, surround myself with varied textures and try new foods. All ideas come from the universal creative flow.

Reframe the Hallway

If you feel stressed and helpless, it may be that you need to work on reframing habits that undermine your progress. Resisting this natural phase indicates that there are unresolved fears or limitations in our thinking, or other barriers inhibiting our growth. It could be that we haven't fully integrated the emotions attached to our choices or we're not being patient enough with ourselves.

If addictions have blocked our creative energy in the past, our job is to learn to reframe our thoughts and feelings. Sobriety or surrender can help us see that our wounds have interfered with our growth. We have the choice to move on from fear, hurt, sadness or anger, into trusting that our lives will improve. We then believe, create and manifest the new. Now is the time to trust divine timing, before our new truth becomes known. If we think back to the beginning of this change, we can ask ourselves if we have fully worked through the first choice, *letting go of the past*. Then we ask ourselves if we have *explored* and reframed our loss into an opportunity and gained sufficient motivation through *talking to others* to help us welcome the new experience. Be patient and gentle as you develop new habits within yourself. Fresh growth takes time.

Paul, a 34-year-old math teacher, came into therapy with his wife because he felt betrayed and confused when he learned she'd been flirting with his "best" friend. But Paul had been obsessing for years about his fear that she'd abandon him, just like his mother, who walked out on his dad a decade earlier. Paul would often get so worked up that he'd become verbally insulting, making his wife feel unloved.

Paul began to work on his unresolved grief over his mother and issues of mistrust. As he confided his fears of abandonment to his wife, he recognized the thought patterns that kept him stuck in the past. By recalling positive memories and experiences with his wife and mother, he was able to connect with the love that he was in fact receiving. Several times throughout the day he affirmed his wife's affection, and in time he realized that she had no need to find validation elsewhere when he expressed his trust and showered her with positive attention.

Reframing these common dilemmas to add new habits of trust may be helpful:

Old Thought	Reframe As:
The habit of thinking, "I don't know what to do."	*I know what to do and I'll sit quietly and ask my higher power to guide me.*
I have not yet opened to my creativity.	*My creativity is bubbling to the surface and I am now discovering healthy expressions.*
If only I could have somehow stopped ___. Now things are worse than ever	*I'm not in charge of the universe, and I can't stop the· process of change. What's done is done. I must remember that it's always darkest before the dawn.*
I don't care what you say, I won't forgive you for the grief I've had to go through as a result of your actions.	*I choose forgiveness and faith. What's done is done. I reclaim my power from the past.*

As we reframe our thoughts, behavior and routines, we integrate our current change with all that we've learned. We begin to feel lighter and have bursts of creativity. During these high points, we get a glimpse of the light at the end of the long, dark hallway. The new feeling may last for only a few hours or days, but it's a start. Of course we want it to be as accessible as a light switch and as lasting as the sun. But we're not there yet. Like a new language, it takes time and practice to become proficient at creating a new reality. For a while you'll stumble back and forth, thinking and speaking in your old negative jargon as well as your new language of confidence.

Continue to revisit the earlier choices until you overcome each challenge. To maintain our actions, we evolve into our new selves, and the gift of our creative energy begins to sparkle with glimpses of hope. Like anything new, the energy bursts forth, recedes and then comes forward again until it is longer lasting. Once we've developed a foundation of trust and good feelings about the world and ourselves, change becomes easier and life seems more predictable.

One morning I woke up and was aware of something being different. My hope returned, I felt courageous, and knew deep within my soul that there was another way to resolve the challenges of change. I began to act on the things that were on my list. Each person I spoke with helped me gather evidence of my progress. It all started to make sense how one experience, person or action was linked to another. *We are all connected.*

When we stay with the choices, we get into motion. We find our courage. Through taking action again and again in the right direction, we learn that this is the way to continue. We start an exercise program. We buy nicotine patches to help us quit smoking. We eat our fruit and vegetables and treat junk food as a treat, not a major food group. We talk to our sponsor, a therapist, career counselor or pastor to get additional support. Hooray! Life supports us after all. We begin to see the light.

Co-Create the New

Motivate yourself by creating new habits through pleasurable images. One habit I decided to change was the concept that life is a struggle. I'd always approached everything with an all-or-nothing, wrestle-em-to-the floor intensity. I was an only daughter with three brothers who kept me hopping. I had to grab what was mine and hold on for dear life. I believed that if I didn't squeeze the thing or experience tightly, it would slip away or be taken from me. As an adult I thought intense (which usually means angst-filled) relationships were better, and working 'til I dropped was more fulfilling. As I think back to the list of fear-based characteristics, I was simply recreating the intensity of my rough-and-tumble family life.

As in many families, we had a lot of stress in our home. Throughout the years I've seen varying levels of family stress and a variety of ways people handle it. I often ask people to plot their family tension on a 100-point scale, with 0 being no stress (impossible for anyone with a pulse) and 100 being off-the-charts unbearable. Family dynamics naturally create tension and conflict and it's our task to find ways to reduce the pressure generated by different needs, priorities, personalities and roles. We laugh, cry, tell stories, play games, create relationships with pets, tease and roughhouse with each other.

If we grow up in a stress-filled environment, we tend to re-create that level of stress again in our adult lives. If our stress level frequently reached 90, then the family tension was set to that level. In some families where people have faith that things will work for the good, the level is usually no higher than 40-50. Those who are raised with attitudes, beliefs and behaviors that resolve tension quickly usually recreate families with lower stress levels. We unconsciously create our old familiar stress patterns because it's all we've known. But when we act *consciously*, using our power of choice, we can visualize new habits that reduce stress. With time, awareness and practice, we can lower the set point to a comfortable level.

Margaret reduced her work schedule to six hours a day to lower the tension in her family. Tom goes for a long walk at lunchtime, and Sylvia goes to her ceramics classes and voice lessons after work to transform her tension into creative expression. My friend Wilna now chooses not to get attached to people's problems, gossip and negative news, and she tries not to overextend herself. She visualizes those she sponsors in her 12-step program, discovering solutions to their challenges, and imagines others learning that gossip is like a boomerang. She visualizes herself balanced and calm throughout her days as she works and takes care of her two daughters.

Using our imagination can be a turning point. Remember, a change can always be a move up the spiritual ladder with the choices of Fearless Change. The power of love embraces us as we accept ourselves and nurture our thoughts, bodies, homes and relationships. It is here that we come to know sacred moments, feel inspired or glimpse a miracle. We are excited about our new insights, optimistic about our creativity and feel the power of spirit co-creating opportunities in our lives. It was wise old Confucius who said, *"I hear and I forget; I see and I remember, I do and I understand."* ➤

Chapter 11

Choose to Be Open to Growth

"We are the beneficiaries of those who dreamed and moved forward, overcoming fear and finding strength."

—Rabbi Robert T. Gan

If you are reading this book, you should know that I made a commitment to follow through and get it published. Many years ago I promised myself to keep meditating, visualizing and affirming a new life. I then made a commitment to my higher power that I would write a book to share the experience of healing. Only I had no idea how to approach it. I looked at a variety of books and wondered if I could even begin to compete. I wimped out and started thinking it might be more efficient if I just kept sending clients to the bookstore to pick up any number of excellent works already in print. But the gnawing wouldn't go away. You can't really bargain with God, but I did say I would do it after my daughter was born.

I needed a compelling reason to put so much effort into an endeavor that was difficult and time-consuming. So several years ago I started writing. First I composed a rough draft about how my daughter was born and about my relationship with her surrogate mother. Then I got sidetracked and decided to write and present training programs for my clients and community businesses. I did some training on the subjects of change, communication, dealing with difficult people and living in balance, but that didn't seem to satisfy me either. I wanted to quit writing, but my commitment to God and myself kept me slaving away at the computer. Whenever I got cross-eyed with fatigue and convinced that I couldn't write my way out of a paper bag, my husband (I think he's really my muse), would tell me, "Keep trying, honey. Winston Churchill said in his autobiography that at first his book was like a lover, then it became a demanding mistress, and finally a taskmaster."

Under my breath I said, "Maybe that's what drove him to smoke cigars." But with my husband's encouragement, I kept pounding away at my keyboard.

As a working mom who gets distracted by a cool breeze, there was always something competing for my attention. *Clean me, repair me, cook me, sew me, play with me and call me* were always options. Finding balance during this process has been interesting. To uncover my voice and get my inner thoughts down on paper wasn't easy, but as soon as I realized I was actually wrenching the message out of my distracted mind and well-intentioned soul, I knew I would finish. Commitment comes anew each day as I sit down to write.

We have all kept commitments to ourselves, to our higher power. And sometimes we've made promises and broken them. Back when I was addicted to some person or substance, I wasn't able to keep commitments to myself, and my self-esteem slipped. At other times I took on more than I could handle and made well-intentioned but impossible promises, then fell short on the follow-through. Today, I know that if I do nothing else but keep my commitments to others as well as myself, my life will run pretty smoothly.

When adapting to change becomes difficult and we can't seem to find the stepping-stones from the Path of Fear to the Path of Trust, we're tempted to quit. Think about your life right now. What commitment did you make to yourself that brought you to this point? Did you promise you'd get well—no matter what? That you would find a job, fulfill a soul contract, live with purpose, stay in your relationship and find your assertive voice to work through your differences? Or did you promise yourself you'd never be treated like *that* again? The commitment required in choice five is the promise we make to ourselves to live out the vision of our change. When we're open and committed to our healing, recovery or to the *new* in our lives, we follow through, no matter what the obstacles. We live the leap of faith as we reframe thoughts and images and reinvent our lives.

Some commitments are easy to keep and others are more difficult. If we've completed the previous four choices, it means we've let go of what is no longer, explored and defined our options, developed positive support and added habits that work for us. Our commitments, though, keep us on track.

Eventually we arrive at this choice of Fearless Change: to be *open to growth* through commitment to our vision, risk-taking and maintaining balance. Until we have sufficient evidence that this new direction is best for us, we vacillate in our decision without wanting to commit. We may want to break our agreements, and we may violate our own values and act without integrity, denying the promises we make to ourselves. Or we may just feel uncertain, trying out the new, comparing it with the old, as we begin to imagine the future with a certain way of being, person, job or creative idea. A new relationship might have some of the qualities you've always wanted yet you miss the comfort of your old flawed-but-familiar companionship. You've arrived at your 90-day review and you can choose to go back to your old position or commit to the new one. Your new job might pay more but perhaps your new colleagues are less compatible. You want to keep moving forward, yet hesitation stops you in your tracks. We know the situation won't last forever, because our awareness will be transformed into yet another event, into something we can't even imagine right now. Change goes on and on, dynamic, eternal and usually unpredictable.

To take healthy risks we need to look beyond the restraint voiced by our inner self or the fears of others. At times we have enormous faith and enthusiasm, and the next minute we're paralyzed by waves of self-doubt. With commitment we listen from within and know we're on the right path. We're inspiredby those who've transcended their own self-imposed limitations.

During our recovery we commit to letting others guide us, and we get new ideas through meetings, sponsors, support groups and our higher power. Eventually we must go within our own hearts and souls to listen to our inner guidance. We commit to taking good care of our bodies, minds, spirits and emotions. With commitment to the new, we attract people who reflect our newfound strength and energy.

An example of the power of commitment can be seen in one of my clients. Steve used to let people and situations overwhelm him. He was angry and depressed, and seemed to be a magnet for others who were also in the grip of negative emotions. He had been reliving the toxic messages from his childhood—and felt worthless. As an adult, he still believed those soul-crippling words, and his employer, reflecting Steve's perceptions, essentially told him the same thing. When Steve was able to overcome his limited thinking, he was able to see life as a wonderful and insightful journey of change. With a clear mind he realized that he needed to make amends to his ex-girlfriend and take financial and emotional responsibility for a child he had fathered many years before. Making contact with his son, who was now nine years old, allowed him to become the kind of father he wished he'd grown up with.

The last time I saw Steve, he and his son, now a teenager, were spending quality time together, both of them grateful for Steve's ability to commit to the process of positive growth to make the choices of Fearless Change. Steve's self-esteem flourished because he was able to keep his commitment to himself. As he reached the point of believing he had worth because he committed and followed through when it counted, he no longer drew negative comments or attracted undesirable friends.

As we practice the fifth choice of Fearless Change, committed to be *open to growth*, we continue to create positive images, gain knowledge, and stay receptive. We see our experiences as opportunities for learning more about ourselves.

Challenge of Commitment

At times we may have a conflict in committing to the new. Both positive and negative images of the outcome dance through our mind and vie for center stage. In the past we may have kept our commitments out of misplaced or fear-based loyalty, but now we have the knowledge to empower ourselves. We can create a list of pros and cons to help us evaluate the rationale of continuing with each commitment. And we can listen to the wisdom of our heart.

Without commitment we'll return to the pain of earlier loss or to our old comfortable ways of dealing with life. After Nora reached her desired weight, she slipped back into over-eating. But she'd learned to *be open* and she continued to create balance, positive images and follow-through, one day at a time. She realized that a target weight is approximate and the result of a healthy, balanced lifestyle. Today she sets daily goals to meet her physical needs and maintains her enthusiasm.

At times our resistance stems from our fear of succeeding and the vulnerability we may experience. We may procrastinate in making a change because we're not that motivated to gain new habits and routines. Our "to do list" isn't enough to motivate us, or we habitually sabotage organizing the house, office or garage even though to have our things more streamlined would make our lives easier. We may say we want love in our lives, yet begin the mental reject list from the first meeting. The fear of success or the fear of failure keeps countless people trapped in the earlier choices of change. We may get the ideas, the creative energy begins to flow, but our belief systems tell us that what we want is impossible. Or once we reach a certain goal, we stop, thinking that we "have it made," and don't ever need to set new goals. Or perhaps our family or friends, limited by *their* own beliefs, tell us that the idea we came up with won't work. And it's often easier in the short run to believe someone else rather than giving ourselves the chance to grow in the vision of our own life. Our thoughts and ideas dictate what we will or won't do.

Actions for Growth

Try this:

Take a moment to look at the following list. Identify the trust or fear-based characteristics that you feel you're committed to. Think about whether or not these are helping you in the long run, not just for today's challenge. We are all committed to something. Are you making choices today that support your commitment to your highest good?

Place a check next to the characteristics that seem to best describe you today. If they are positive—that's great. If they are based in fear/guilt/remorse, and are not something you want to experience any longer, take the time now to write out your thoughts and beliefs which are fearful and re-write them in the positive. Keep writing until you are able to embrace a trusting, loving and pleasurable based belief. You may need to spend more time on some of these characteristics however, by reframing your perceptions will enhance your mood and increase your self esteem. Pick up your pen and start feeling better right now!

Fear / Shame / Pain	Trust / Love / Pleasure
Resistance	Growth
Resentments	Forgiveness
Visualizing failure	Visualizing success
Isolating	Spending time with others
Scarcity	Prosperity
Withholding	Giving
Rejection	Affection
Time focus — future or the past	Time focus — Now
Deception	Truth
Control	Cooperation
Illusion	Reality
Judgment	Acceptance
Self-Centeredness	Consideration of others
Guilt	Innocence
Responsibility for others	Responsibility to others
Chaos	Serenity
Giving up	Follow-through
Reactive	Responsive
Defensive	Vulnerable

Daily Decisions

Decisions recast our relationships, work environments, income, or physical and emotional well-being. It's the small decisions we make each day that contribute to success or failure in everything we do. It's these choices that determine whether we're happy or sad, frustrated or excited, feeling trapped or free. Now is the time to make decisions about what we stand for and what is acceptable or unacceptable in our lives.

Joanne, a woman who lives in my neighborhood and is something of a local philanthropist, told me that she gave away her savings many years ago to help someone start a business, without any thought of it being an investment. She thought that helping someone's creative expression was more important than her own financial security. But in time she felt guilt and shame for not taking better care of herself. The business eventually failed and she was never repaid. She wasn't committed to *her* life, and was overly committed to someone else's. As her healing and recovery increased, she accepted her own worth, and came to understand Shakespeare's saying, *"To thine own self be true."* Giving a budgeted amount to charity fulfilled her need to share with others, without undermining her own well-being.

Committing to Fearless Change

With the Fearless Change process we commit to the needs of our soul. The goal of the fifth choice is to make a commitment to the new as a result of the changes we've experienced. As we come closer to integrating our change we go forward with increased trust and faith.

The ongoing recovery from addiction, spiritual deprivation, trauma, divorce, illness, career change or the death of a loved one all require one thing: a commitment to ourselves to live to the fullest—each day. It requires that we replace apathy with enthusiasm and seek pleasure instead of pain, and love instead of fear.

When we commit, we promise to ourselves to use our personal resources in order to follow through with our plans. We establish a relationship with our spiritual source, ask questions, and if we're really committed to live out our truth, we follow its guidance. We commit our resources—including our positive energy, strongly held beliefs, time, money, relationships, careers or lifestyles. We commit to sticking with our decisions to grow and learn even when our mood or resolve fluctuates.

As a result, we naturally move on and choose to *discover the benefits*. To succeed we rely on the strength of our inner discipline, which we have developed through our empowering habits and the choices of Fearless Change. Eleanor Roosevelt described this decision in the following manner: *"You must do the things you think you cannot do."* ➤

Chapter 12

Choose to Discover Benefits

*"If we took responsibility for our freedom, committed ourselves to
service, and had faith that our security lay within...
we could stop asking the question
'How?' We would see that we have the answer."*

--Peter Block, *Stewardship*

To *discover the benefits*, we commit to reframing the challenges
that occur with change. We now have the opportunity to pull
it all together and reap the rewards of our efforts: We keep our
balance, stay grateful, give back and get involved. Our new
foundation is in our awakened intuition, spiritual connection and
creativity. We become conscious of our thoughts and creative
ideas flow easily. We think in terms of solutions and trust spirit to
reveal them. Life challenges become simply problems to be
solved. There is always an answer, if you keep recommitting to
the process. We have learned to accept that challenges are here for
our highest good. We take action to reach our goals, one step at a
time. No matter what the test, the Fearless Change Map shows us
that by choosing to discover benefits we celebrate our transitions.
And through our gratitude and service to others we open our
hearts to love and compassion and we all benefit.

As we step forward we thank the persons or experiences
that were instrumental in our change. We discover even more

gifts when we send a note of thanks, make a phone call or offer a small gift to express our gratitude. We feel fulfilled when we share our experience with others, and state the direction of our journey.

Coming Full Circle

This is a time when we give back in service and participation. Service opportunities give us a chance to express our values and utilize our gifts. It's also a chance to meet new people who share common interests and stimulate our intellectual, creative and social growth.

If we don't discover the benefits and give back to others, we're apt to become boastful, angry and even relapse back to our old ways. If our hurt feelings and unwillingness to forgive have not been expressed, the resentments will eat away at our body and soul.

Healing is never complete unless we complete the circle and share it with others. From the courage and love we've gained as a result of our change, we become the mothers, fathers, leaders, supervisors, teachers, mentors and healers that we set out to become. Whether our contribution is to our families, neighbors, 12-step programs, volunteer work or professional associations, by giving back we help others and ourselves. To become whole is the gift of our giving.

Bumps along the Way

The goal of Fearless Change — to embrace the choice to reinvent our life — is to identify those feelings, beliefs or communication patterns that either move us forward or give us feet of clay. If we don't feel ready to show appreciation for the events that stimulated our growth, we need to return to the first choice of Fearless Change. As you accept the past, amend an action or forgive someone who has blocked your growth, it's time to again move through the next choice. Your sense of peace is the only way to determine if you've integrated these decisions in your life. Since processes are fluid and dynamic, we may find ourselves going two steps forward and one step back. Sometimes we compare our progress to that of others, and therefore incorrectly judge how far we've come.

Not everyone makes it through the process of change in the same time frame or in exactly the same way. Where one person might see a job layoff as a traumatic loss, his or her partner might view it as the opportunity of a lifetime. When we live with others, we see that each person has a unique time for growing and changing, or staying stuck.

Some people are unable to overcome the grief of what *was* in their lives. They carry around the shreds of lost love, family, career or wealth, resentful of *whoever* or *whatever* caused their loss. Others, like a football star whose career peaks with an 80-yard run, don't just grieve for the *way it was – they glorify it.* The good old days are relived time and again, self-esteem hanging by a slender thread. Some of us have been so wounded by earlier traumas that love, trust, acceptance and growth seem almost impossible. To explore the new is threatening to the fragile status quo. It may seem safer to stagnate than to soar. And then there are some of us who stumble through the choice of *discovering the benefits* because the new relationship, friend or job hits a bump, so we fear it's over and cut our losses before giving it a fair chance. What we don't realize is that the unlearned lesson will be presented again and again, until we learn to follow through. What bumps keep reappearing in your life?

Changed

Once we choose to *discover the benefits*, we forget what we went through in the process of reinventing our lives. We now pay attention to our choices and decisions, our intuition, and trust our direction and pace. We are grateful, we celebrate the moments, pray, meditate and continue to gather support. We meet our needs, and know how to reframe and reinvent our choices if we end up on the Path of Fear. We explore new avenues by reading books, talking to others, getting involved with our communities, attending meetings and workshops, and continuing to learn. We choose to feed our souls with vital awareness and creativity.

As a result, we spend our days on the Path of Trust and we feel valued because we have honored ourselves. We are grateful and feel our vitality overflow. We want to help others individually and contribute to society. James volunteers at his community center. Marianne hosts a drop-in group in her home. Eric serves on his employee club membership committee and Louise sponsors newcomers into her 12-step group. By offering to mentor a new person in the workplace, coaching youth sports or helping a child in need, we discover our appreciation for the process of life.

Giving back helps us to remain humble, grateful, flexible and receptive. We realize that the integration of our change is a gift. As we maintain our balance, we share our joy with others and we feel more expansive. As we continue to learn, we sustain our accomplishments, and that becomes a foundation for further change.

Life is dynamic and ever evolving. Each of us is in a constant state of renewal in some aspect of our existence. Remember that what we give away comes back to us. As we serve others we are creating an easier road the next time we're visited by a major change. When you give of your smile, when you appreciate and empathize with others, you help heal the universe more than you might realize. We all need your inspiration and support to remind us that change can indeed be fearless. To remember the six choices of Fearless Change, just keep this in mind:

L   Let go of what is no longer.

E   Explore options.

T   Talk to others.

G   Gain healthy habits.

O   Open yourself to growth.

D   Discover the benefits.

"What we call the beginning is often the end. And to make our end is to make a beginning. The end is where we start from." — T.S. Elliott ➤

INDEX

About the Author

Judy Saalinger is a licensed marriage, family therapist and certified addiction specialist in private practice in San Diego, California. She has been helping individuals, families and the community to embrace change and reinvent their lives since 1981. She offers workshops and training on the process of change and is available for individual consultations, radio talk shows and speaking engagements. Dr. Saalinger can be contacted through www.lastingrecovery.com, by calling 800-808-6373, or writing to her at Lasting Recovery, 6046 Cornerstone Court W. #112, San Diego, CA 92121.

Learn more about FEARLESS CHANGE
Additional Products and Services

Contact us at 800-808-6373

Publications
___ FEARLESS CHANGE *Embrace the Choice to Reinvent Your Life,* Audio Book Edition
___ FEARLESS CHANGE Guidebook
___ Fearless Change Map – laminated – varying sizes
___ Choices of Change Chart – laminated – varying sizes

For Professionals
___ FEARLESS CHANGE WORKSHOP SERIES – A 12 week structured program designed for Alcohol and Drug Recovery facilities – inpatient, outpatient and residential. Includes a training workshop, detailed facilitators guide, overheads and handouts.

Name_____

Address _____

City _____ State____   Zip_____

E-mail Address: _____

Phone # ( ) _____ FAX ( ) _____

Want to share your story of change? Tell us how you benefited from the process of FEARLESS CHANGE. An upcoming book, now being compiled!

Send to: Lasting Recovery Publications
6046 Cornerstone Court W. #112, San Diego, CA 92121
800-808-6373   FAX: 858-453-5690
e-mail: Judy@lastingrecovery.com